SO-ACQ-993

Plough Quarterly

BREAKING GROUND FOR A RENEWED WORLD

Autumn 2020, Number 25

Feature: Solidarity

Essays and Poetry

Reviews and Profiles

Plough Quarterly

WWW.PLOUGH.COM

Meet the community behind *Plough*

Plough Quarterly is published by the Bruderhof, an international community of families and singles seeking to follow Jesus together. Members of the Bruderhof are committed to a way of radical discipleship in the spirit of the Sermon on the Mount. Inspired by the first church in Jerusalem (Acts 2 and 4), they renounce private property and share everything in common in a life of nonviolence, justice, and service to neighbors near and far. The community includes people from a wide range of backgrounds. There are twenty-three Bruderhof settlements in both rural and urban locations in the United States, England, Germany, Austria, Australia, Paraguay, and South Korea, with around 3,000 people in all. To learn more or arrange a visit, see the community's website at *bruderhof.com*.

Plough Quarterly features original stories, ideas, and culture to inspire everyday faith and action. Starting from the conviction that the teachings and example of Jesus can transform and renew our world, we aim to apply them to all aspects of life, seeking common ground with all people of goodwill regardless of creed. The goal of *Plough Quarterly* is to build a living network of readers, contributors, and practitioners so that, in the words of Hebrews, we may "spur one another on toward love and good deeds." *Plough Quarterly* includes contributions that we believe are worthy of our readers' consideration, whether or not we fully agree with them. Views expressed by contributors are their own and do not necessarily reflect the editorial position of *Plough* or of the Bruderhof communities.

Editor: Peter Mommsen. Senior Editors: Maureen Swinger, Sam Hine. Editor-at-Large: Caitrin Keiper. Managing Editor: Shana Goodwin. Associate Editors: Susannah Black, Ian Barth. Designers: Rosalind Stevenson, Miriam Burleson. Creative Director: Clare Stober. Copy Editors: Wilma Mommsen, Priscilla Jensen. Fact Checker: Emmy Barth Maendel. Marketing Director: Trevor Wiser. International Editions: Kim Comer (German), Chungyon Won (Korean), Allen Page (French). Founding Editor: Eberhard Arnold (1883–1935).

Plough Quarterly No. 25: Solidarity
Published by Plough Publishing House, ISBN 978-0-87486-354-3
Copyright © 2020 by Plough Publishing House. All rights reserved.

Scripture quotations (unless otherwise noted) are from the New Revised Standard Version Bible, copyright © 1989 the Division of Christian Education of the National Council of the Churches of Christ in the United States of America. Used by permission. All rights reserved. Front cover: Artwork by Rosalind Stevenson; image used with permission. Inside front cover: Fritz Eichenberg, *Christ of the Breadlines*, wood engraving, 1953; image © Fritz Eichenberg Trust. Back cover: John August Swanson, *Festival of Lights*, serigraph, 1991; image from Wikimedia (public domain). Back cover text: Eberhard Arnold, address on June 2, 1935 (Bruderhof Historical Archive, EA 35/59), trans. Hugo Brinkmann.

Editorial Office	*Subscriber Services*	*United Kingdom*	*Australia*
151 Bowne Drive	PO Box 345	Brightling Road	4188 Gwydir Highway
Walden, NY 12586	Congers, NY 10920-0345	Robertsbridge	Elsmore, NSW
T: 845.572.3455	T: 800.521.8011	TN32 5DR	2360 Australia
info@plough.com	subscriptions@plough.com	T: +44(0)1580.883.344	T: +61(0)2.6723.2213

Plough Quarterly (ISSN 2372-2584) is published quarterly by Plough Publishing House, PO Box 398, Walden, NY 12586. Individual subscription $32 / £24 / €28 per year. Subscribers outside the United Kingdom and European Union pay in US dollars. Periodicals postage paid at Walden, NY 12586 and at additional mailing offices.
POSTMASTER: Send address changes to *Plough Quarterly*, PO Box 345, Congers, NY 10920-0345.

Solidarity in Forgiveness

PETER MOMMSEN

Dear Reader,

PANDEMICS, WHATEVER ELSE they do, show us we are not alone. "No man is an island," runs the much-quoted John Donne line, and that never seems truer than when you're trying to be an island and failing: not keeping six feet of distance when meeting a friend, fighting to get the kids to keep their masks on, simmering with resentment that you can't get to a Mets game.

Covid-19 is proof that, yes, there *is* such a thing as society; the disease has spread precisely because we aren't autonomous individuals disconnected from each other, but rather all belong to one great body of humanity. The pain inflicted by the pandemic is far from equally distributed. Yet it reveals ever more clearly how much we all depend on one another, and how urgently necessary it is for us to bear one another's burdens. Faced with the dilemma of how to resume social interactions safely, we've learned how badly we miss each other. In a way unimaginable a year ago, seven billion people's joys and tears – at least in regard to the spread of the virus while we await a vaccine – are our own.

It's a good time, then, to talk about solidarity. The more so because it's a theme that's also raised by this year's other major development, the international protests for racial justice following George Floyd's death. It was astonishing to watch crowds chanting "Black Lives Matter" in cities as far removed from

> "Everyone is really responsible to everyone for everyone and for everything."
>
> Fyodor Dostoyevsky

US policing as Stockholm, Seville, and Sydney. Here was solidarity, or at least a craving for something resembling it.

The protests, too, raised the question of solidarity in guilt, even guilt across generations. One demand voiced by many protesters was for reparations: that the descendants of slavery's perpetrators and beneficiaries pay back a debt to the descendants of the enslaved. How this would work in practice is far from clear, yet even critics of the idea will agree that in principle, reparations can be a just response to historical wrongs. Millions of Germans born after 1945 continue to pay reparations through their tax money to the descendants of those their great-grandparents killed. Truth and reconciliation initiatives in South Africa and elsewhere have sought to provide a kind of intergenerational justice. And in the United States, this year the Supreme Court reached back to an 1833 treaty to recognize half of Oklahoma as Native tribal land, in a ruling referencing the country's appalling atrocities against Native Americans. In varying ways, each of these examples involves a claim about inherited responsibility – and perhaps inherited guilt.

Built into these claims is a logic at which the liberal mind angrily recoils. Schooled to think only in terms of individual rights and responsibilities, it asks: How can I be held responsible for evils over which I have no control?

Many Christians might be inclined to agree with the objection. But the Christian tradition says: not so fast. In fact, Christianity takes solidarity in guilt, even inherited guilt, with utmost seriousness. According to the apostle Paul, all humankind sinned and was condemned in the sin of our forefather Adam: "For as in Adam all die . . . " (1 Cor. 15). Whether one speaks of "original sin" with Augustine, "federal headship" with the Reformers, or "total Adam" with Orthodox thinkers, this is not a theme Christians are free to casually dismiss.

The most vivid exploration of this kind of solidarity is Fyodor Dostoyevsky's novel *The Brothers Karamazov*. Dostoyevsky has one character, a dying teenager, tell his mother: "Every one of us has sinned against all men. . . . Everyone is really responsible to all men for all men and for everything."

Responsibility for all and to all: on its face, this seems nonsensical. Its logic tars each of us with the guilt not only of those whom we know and might theoretically influence, but also with the sins of people we'll never meet and of people long dead. (A cynic might add that responsibility for everything amounts, in the real world, to responsibility for nothing.)

Yet Dostoyevsky's words aren't just the ruminations of an eccentric novelist. They are repeated almost verbatim in one of the towering statements of modern Christian social teaching, Pope John Paul II's 1987 encyclical *Sollicitudo rei socialis* (see page 56). Solidarity, the pope writes, "is not a feeling of vague compassion or shallow distress at the misfortunes of so many people, both near and far. On the contrary, it is a firm and persevering determination to commit oneself to the common good; that is to say, to the good of all and of each individual, because we are all really responsible for all."

THIS TRUE SOLIDARITY is the opposite of the false solidarities of today's identity politics on both the right and the left. Whether simply racist or purportedly antiracist, such false solidarities regard people primarily as bearers of one or more group identities based on nationality, race, class, or gender – and view these identity groups as inevitably antagonistic, locked with other groups in a bitter struggle for power. Here, "justice" means little more than a tense balancing of group interests. As a result, those who embrace such a worldview are liable to make recourse to coercion and even violence, as ugly episodes at some of the protests this past summer illustrate.

By contrast, Christianity – with Judaism and other faiths – teaches that people are first and foremost bearers of the divine image. Each of us shares with all others the fundamental bond of our common humanity. Because of this, the gospel utterly condemns the oppression of one group by another, including the entire demonic edifice of white supremacy (see page 30). But for the same reason, it refuses to fight fire with fire, combating group self-interest with group self-interest. Instead, it offers the way of solidarity in guilt of which John Paul II and Dostoyevsky speak.

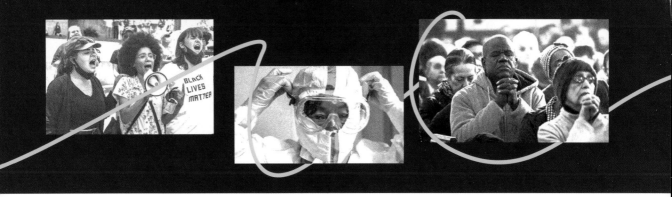

This way is no grim invitation to endless self-abasing struggle sessions. (In this, it couldn't differ more from the racial essentialism of best-sellers such as Robin DiAngelo's *White Fragility*.) Instead, it is a doorway to rediscovering the glorious calling we share with all human beings.

By taking up our common guilt with all humanity, we come into solidarity with the one who bears it and redeems it all. "For as in Adam all die," Paul continues, "even so in Christ shall all be made alive." In Christ, sins are forgiven, guilt abolished, and a new way of living together becomes possible.

This solidarity in forgiveness – the solidarity that Christ has taken up with us – gives rise to a life of love. It's the reason why another character in *The Brothers Karamazov* could say: "As for each man being guilty before all and for all, besides his own sins . . . when people understand this thought, the kingdom of heaven will come to them, no longer a dream but in reality."

ONE HUNDRED YEARS AGO this year, in a Germany shattered by war and revolution, a discussion group met each Thursday evening in a townhouse in Berlin to imagine a new way to live, one shaped by this kind of solidarity. As Antje Vollmer describes (page 98), the young participants were a diverse bunch: evangelicals and anarchists, military officers and pacifists, artists and Quakers. In a country ruined by nationalism, militarism, and exploitation, Dostoyevsky's words about responsibility for all and to all struck them with enormous force. Especially, they read

Jesus' Sermon on the Mount. There, they found a God who invites us to a practical, creative way of life in which our solidarity in guilt is transformed into a new kind of togetherness as we work side by side to build the new social order the Gospels describe.

At the end of one of their gatherings in the spring of 1920, a young woman stood up and announced: "We have talked enough. Now it is time for deeds." Eberhard and Emmy Arnold, the couple hosting the evenings, took her words to heart. He resigned his job at a Christian publishing house and sold his life insurance policy; Emmy brought their five children to a dilapidated villa in the backwater village of Sannerz. Together with Emmy's sister Else von Hollander, they founded a communal settlement inspired by the example of the first Christians, and with friends started a new publishing house with the name *Neuwerk:* the New Work. Over the following decades, the publishing house would take the English name Plough, and the communal settlement would become the Bruderhof, the community that publishes this magazine (see page 102).

In the same spirit as the Berlin discussion group a century ago, this issue of *Plough* seeks to explore what solidarity means, and what it looks like to live it out today, whether in Uganda, Bolivia, or South Korea, in an urban church, a Bruderhof, or a convent. We look forward to hearing what you think.

Warm greetings,

Peter

Peter Mommsen, *Editor*

Ministers and Magistrates

On John D. Roth's "The Anabaptist Vision of Politics," Spring 2020: In Romans 13, after he has enumerated our temporal duties – "Pay all of them their dues, taxes to whom taxes are due, revenue to whom revenue is due, respect to whom respect is due . . ." – Saint Paul unexpectedly reveals that *all* these obligations, and not just the law written upon our hearts, are fulfilled by the precept of charity. "Owe no one anything, except to love one another; for he who loves his neighbor has fulfilled the law." Love is enough. The coercive power of the temporal ruler should have no business with the Christian.

And when it comes to the infliction of such force it seems the Lord leaves little room to the spiritual power. As he told Pilate, "My kingdom is not of this world. If my kingdom were of this world, my servants would certainly strive that I should not be delivered to the Jews: but now my kingdom is not from hence." And to the mob he says, "He that is without sin among you, let him cast the first stone."

Thus far, the vision of Anabaptist political theology is quite correct. And the force of this vision should not be watered down. But what of those who obstinately place themselves outside the bond of charity? What of he who "will not hear the church" who is to "be to thee as the heathen and publican"? And what if this occurs in a manner "that is not tolerated even among pagans"? What provision has God made in this case?

Saint Paul has a severe mercy in their regard. While he forbids the Christians of Corinth to "go to law before the unrighteous" *with each other*, he has no such scruple in regard to the

excommunicate (1 Cor. 5): "I have already pronounced judgment in the name of the Lord Jesus on the man who has done such a thing. When you are assembled, and my spirit is present, with the power of our Lord Jesus, you are to deliver this man to Satan [that is, excommunicate him, so that he could then be given up to the Roman authorities without violating the prohibition on doing such a thing to a brother] for the destruction of the flesh, that his spirit may be saved in the day of the Lord Jesus." Salvation is still the goal, but the obstinate one is surrendered to temporal coercion.

Thus, Constantine called himself "a bishop, ordained by God to oversee those outside the church." But delivery to Satan and the emperor's destruction of the flesh are not synonymous. Those forces were allied – have often been allied – but the connection is not necessary. If it *were* necessary, it would not be culpable; Caesar *need not be* the quasi-Satanic figure he is in some of the New Testament; the government need not be as compromised with evil as Rome was.

We pray for rulers so that we may have a peaceful life – and also because God desires

---

We welcome letters to the editor. Letters may be edited for length and clarity, and may be published in any medium. Letters should be sent with the writer's name and address to letters@plough.com.

all to be saved, including kings. Was not Saint Paul God's vessel of election to bear his name before "the Gentiles *and their kings*"? This is, certainly, to announce that the one who is King of Kings, emperor over these subordinate rulers, has come, and to command their allegiance; it is also to invite their reconciliation with him as men, even as they remain in their positions of authority, giving him homage as their high king.

When we stray outside the bond of charity in some respect injurious to the temporal peace – when we steal, or commit murder – we fail to render to God what belongs to him, and we are rightly handed over to Caesar: Caesar has been given power from above (John 19:11), in wielding which he is God's minister (Isa. 60:10), and so we are his debtors too. To be a governor – to be a king – can be, therefore, simply to be obedient to the role to which God has assigned you; to fail in the duty of governing would be to fail in the task which has been entrusted to you.

Alan Fimister, Denver, Colorado

On John Huleatt's "The Bruderhof and the State," Spring 2020: If you know where to look, you'll find magisterial Protestants who admire the radical Anabaptists in a line stretching back to the earliest days of our shared history. The Strasbourg reformer Martin Bucer knew many of the early radicals, routinely engaging them in public debate. After Michael Sattler's martyrdom at the hands of Austrian authorities, Bucer called him a "martyr of Christ."

Indeed, there is much in Bucer's vision of magisterial Protestantism that echoes aspects of radicalism – not least the demand that all followers of Jesus take up the yoke of Christ, living sacrificially for the good of the neighbor.

Yet Bucer remained committed to the magisterial tradition. For Bucer, the call to love one's neighbor was inextricably tied to the work of promoting and advocating for a Christian society more generally, including a Christian state. Advocacy for a Christian social order is one means of promoting the common good in this vision.

This had to be the case, according to Bucer, for the simple reason that we do not pass the entirety of our lives within our local church. The claim that Christ makes on a believer's life extends to all domains. The claims of the visible church, however, do not. And so there was a need to account for the shape Christian discipleship would take in the memberships that we are part of other than our local church.

Defining what this would be was the task the magisterial Protestants set themselves. At our best, as in the model of Bucer, who personally hosted religious refugees from France for the entirety of his marriage and ministry in Strasbourg, this discipleship very much includes the disruptive witness of the radical tradition. But unlike the radicals and unlike the Roman tradition, the magisterial tradition seeks not to draw all the world into the life of the visible church, but rather to see all of life offered up directly to Christ himself.

Jake Meador, Lincoln, Nebraska

American Muslims: Race, Faith, and Political Allegiance

On Shadi Hamid's "Holding Our Own: Is the Future of Islam in the West Communal?" Spring 2020: A sublime piece by Shadi Hamid, who draws attention to the fact that as they have become part of the Democratic coalition, American Muslims have adopted some very liberal positions. But this, Hamid argues, is not the only natural alliance; he argues for common cause between conservative Christians and Muslims.

Is there room for a more genuinely Islamic conservative political and social presence to emerge in the United States? I think there may be. It is possible to imagine a cross-religious coalition on the grounds of cultural values.

Europe is secular, and some of Europe's – especially France's – anti-Muslim sentiment builds on historical anticlericalism and anti-Catholicism. But Europe's inability to tolerate Muslims' worldview and religious observance predates its secularism and has, at least in part, a different origin. Unlike the United States, Europe's identity has always been partially defined in opposition to Islam. Europe is equally unwilling to accept white Muslim immigrants as it is to accept black and brown Muslim immigrants. Its animus is framed in religious, rather than primarily racial, terms.

Hence, Hamid's point that conservative Muslims have a chance to be politically active in the United States and need not accept the Democratic Party's liberal dogma is compelling. It's not just that the United States is less secular than Europe. It also lacks Europe's long history of Islamophobia. There just might be room for a Muslim conservative Republican constituency in the States.

In one of the most interesting and important sections of the piece, Hamid gives voice to Ismael Royer, who hits the nail on the head by criticizing the left's attempt to redefine "Islam as a secular identity group centered on ethnic 'brownness.'" It is much easier to integrate Muslims into the Democratic coalition as people of color than as a religious group. That still doesn't make it intellectually honest, and doesn't serve either of these communities.

The 2020 election cycle has highlighted this issue. The Sanders campaign's main Muslim supporters did exactly what Royer describes: they reduced Muslims to ethnic brownness. But at least one in ten US Muslims is of European origin, and their voices have to be taken into account when discussing the dilemmas Muslims face as a religious and cultural group in the West.

To conclude, Hamid's main point is novel and groundbreaking: American Muslims have a unique opportunity to live in freedom while potentially forging political and social alliances with conservative Christian political actors who share a similar view of morality, society, and the human person.

Reuf Bajrović, Washington, DC

Love's Victory

On Maureen Swinger's "Precious Friend: What's Your Victory Song?" 2020 Special Digital Issue: I'd like to thank you, Maureen, for writing about Robert and his family and friends, as well as earlier about your brother Duane, who also had special needs (*"The Teacher Who Never Spoke," Spring 2017*). There are so many threads holding you and us together in addition to the love of God. I think of your ability to understand the challenges faced by Robert and his family because of what you learned from Duane. Your position of strength comes from having experienced great hardships and challenges. You all clearly are celebrating the life of the beautiful boy Robert, both giving and receiving joy in doing so. We have a good friend who has ALS, and for about a year now he has been able to move only his eyes. I think of the deep inner contemplation and acceptance that those whose movement is inhibited must learn to accept and even embrace. In reading about Robert's sixth birthday serenade with Jean close by, baby daughter in arm, I saw myself as if in a mirror twenty-seven years ago, holding my baby daughter and helping my seven-year-old son, whose movement was severely limited by weakness caused by leukemia. (Our son passed on in 1993. He

is still teaching me.) Child and parents are refined and purified by the suffering of the child. And we have so much to be grateful for. To hold and love such a gift from God is a gift not to be surpassed.

Laurie Brown, Lancaster, Pennsylvania

No Easy Comfort

On Edwidge Danticat's "This Too Shall Pass?" 2020 Special Digital Issue: Thank you, Edwidge Danticat. This is beautiful. We have a much-loved friend who has moved out of home from wife and baby in case of infecting them, due to frontline work. We can't glibly say everything will be all right. But as the Iona Community pray at the end of a communion celebration: "Is God good? God is good. Is life worth living? Life is worth living. Is the best yet to come? Always, the best is yet to come. Then go, as friends of Jesus and enjoy him forever."

Wendy Phillips, Dublin, Ireland

He Did Not Open His Mouth

On Zito Madu's "The Edge of Justice," part of the Arc of Justice series on Plough.com: Madu's piece reminded me of some of the street boys I know in Lima, Peru, from my frequent visits there. Their life is hateful and they are hated by most people. They don't trust anyone. When they are hunted by the police they are abused beyond belief. They are asked to tell about their hideouts and the names of their friends and so forth. They consider "ratting out their friends" the very worst thing they could do. So they keep their silence, and get kicked around like soccer balls by the police.

They usually want nothing to do with the message of Jesus. But one day we were telling them about Jesus' interrogation by the authorities. As the spiritual says, "He never said a mumblin' word" when they struck him and spit on him. A couple of the boys were wide eyed. "He kept his silence," they said. They could relate to that. It was the opening we needed to share the love of Jesus.

You never know what will help people to hear. Jesus lived life completely; every moment of his life can touch someone.

Betty Purchase, Holiday, Florida

Salt and Light to the Warriors

On Ronald J. Sider's "Christian Nonviolence and Church History," on Plough.com: Sider quotes Miroslav Volf: "If one decides to put on soldier's gear instead of carrying one's cross, one should not seek legitimation in the religion that worships the crucified Messiah." Later, Sider says that "no extant Christian text from before Constantine says military service is ever legitimate."

I struggle with these things. In all the years I've read arguments along these lines, I have never seen anyone grapple to my satisfaction with the narrative of the first Gentile to be converted, "Cornelius, a centurion of what was known as the Italian Cohort, a devout man who feared God with all his household, gave alms generously to the people, and prayed continually to God" (Acts 10:1–2). The only command Peter issued was for him and his companions to be baptized. In this he was following Jesus, who said of a centurion, "I have not found anyone in Israel with such great faith," and who didn't tell him to leave the service (Matt. 8:5–13).

I'm not convinced that military service means one is not and cannot be a true worshiper of the crucified Messiah. There is also no place in such arguments for the thousands of Christians who have served among, ministered to, and witnessed to the military. There are those in the military who mock Jesus – and those who would say, with another centurion, "Truly this was the Son of God!"

Do unbelievers in the military not need salt and light, especially when deployed? My wife is a retired officer who has been salt and light in all of her units. When I once made this argument to a "Volfian," he told me that my wife was a whore justifying it by claiming to be salt and light in a whorehouse. Violence comes in many forms.

I believe I would be compelled by conscience to try to protect another. When I was eleven, I was repeatedly struck in the face by a bully, and intentionally raised no hand to defend myself, but I also stood my ground and allowed him to continue striking me. An older boy stopped it by standing beside me and challenging the bully to fight him. That he stood up for me was, I think, right; that moment, and his courage, has influenced me to this day, and it is why I also believe law enforcement can be conducted by Christians.

I have found that many Christian pacifists seem to think that Christians in the armed forces never struggle with the issue. My wife and I, along with brothers and sisters in Officers' Christian Fellowship in college, read deeply and struggled with this, and I still do. None were ever eager for violence, and while most I knew settled on Just War doctrine, they didn't get there by default.

Likewise, there are deep spiritual struggles for many of us in military families. I opposed the war in Iraq as both a moral evil and a political mistake even as my wife was deployed there twice. Learning how to support someone you love who is in a combat zone is a spiritual challenge.   *Bo Grimes, Burke, Virginia*

A Moment in *Kairos* Time

On Leslie Verner's "The Gift of Death," on Plough.com: This article deeply touched me.

My father and I were not close. Or perhaps we were, but did not know how to show it. The one time we hugged was awkward and we never again risked that discomfort.

I was in the military and he came for a visit. Neither of us had ever seen the mountains, so I took leave and we drove to see the continental divide for the first time. As we came to the top of the pass, the entire horizon of the valley below was backdropped by snow-capped peaks as far as the eye could see in either direction.

I was taken by this *kairos* you speak of in your article: For a moment there was no "me." I was experiencing pure being/God. My personality had no reference point for what I was seeing and it momentarily shut down my thinking mind. I could sense my father's body shaking in the seat next to me and I knew he was having the same experience. He reached out and held my hand. For a moment, there was no distance between us. We were in full communion with each other, God, the mountains . . . all of creation. He said with a shaking voice, "What was that?"

We never talked about that experience, but for the short time he had left, we would look at each other with soft eyes knowing love that goes beyond words. He died shortly thereafter. That was thirty years ago. I ache to have that experience again.

Greg Bourn, Kailua Kona, Hawaii

Casa da Videira's bakers display their wares.

Letter from Brazil: Mutation Time

Claudio Oliver of the Casa da Videira community in Curitiba, Brazil, describes how they are adapting and connecting with neighbors during the pandemic.

Brazil is facing several major challenges at the same time – what we could call the perfect storm. First, like the rest of the world, there is the coronavirus situation. I don't call it a crisis because a crisis is something that crops up and after it you have your life back. It's much more like a mutation time – society is mutating, there's no going back.

At the same time, in our area we are having the worst drought ever recorded in our country – literally no rain in the past six months. The bigger rivers we have in our region are drying – you can actually walk on the riverbeds. This is a direct consequence of the burning in the Amazon forest. With climate change, these problems will continue to get worse.

And to manage these emergencies, we have an abusive and incompetent government, widely recognized by international media as one of the worst in the world.

But internally within our community we are happy, because we have time to share life with our brothers and sisters. With less social interaction, our relationships are becoming more essential. We are urban gardening, making pasta, and connecting with our neighbors through our business of offering locally produced food. We are finding new ways to serve people with what we know how to do, like baking bread. Through the bread we are connecting to more and more people every week.

We must be aware that we are watching the end of the world as we know it. And we must prevent ourselves from longing for a world that is not there anymore. A good image is Lot's wife. We are not afraid about what is ahead of us; actually, we have been preparing ourselves for this moment for years. Last year, for example, we started thinking about ourselves as a lab or a workshop of proposals for after the end of the world. This is the name of our new movement: A Workshop of Proposals for After the End of the World. We want a future that questions what the world means by normal, in terms of economics, politics, families, and

Ravioli made at Casa da Videira

more. We are experimenting for this future from what we are able to do *today*. The future *is* built today.

Read Claudio Oliver's full letter at plough.com/MutationTime.

New Community in South Korea

Helen Huleatt

Two years ago, several Bruderhof members traveled to South Korea to form a new community. Within months, more families joined, and we now number about twenty-five.

Physical community and common work are cherished future dreams. Meanwhile, with other residents, we live in apartment blocks facing one of South Korea's last operating coal mines near the city of Taebaek, not far from our friends at the Jesus Abbey founded by Archer and Jane Torrey. Several members have jobs locally; others care for children and household tasks. We meet as often as we can.

Our community feels young and fragile. But like the rice growing in nearby valleys, it gains power from above, and we pray it will bear a harvest for God's kingdom. We hope our joyful efforts to care for each other and to build unity will serve our neighbors, the whole land (including North Korea), and the entire world.

Francis Schaeffer and L'Abri

Jake Meador

When I met Dean, he was a widowed, stooped, pipe-smoking, eighty-five-year-old retired journalist living in an RV. We struck up a conversation – I was an aspiring journalist, fascinated by his stories. Like the time he met Jim Morrison before the Doors played a mid-6os concert – "A very polite young man when he was sober," Dean said.

By the darker late 6os, Dean was in a dark place himself. He left California for a newspaper job in St. Louis. On his way into the city, he heard a woman's voice on the radio, reading the news. He decided he wanted to meet her. He did. They quickly fell in love and were married by the only clergyman they knew – their Unitarian-minister pot hookup.

The couple soon discovered that they hoped to find something real in the world, something that could make them believe in good things again. So they traveled to Europe in search of enlightenment. They did not find it.

The last night before returning to America, they ate at a café in Madrid, talking about the disappointing trip. A couple nearby overheard them – "There's a place you should visit in Switzerland,"

Bruderhof community in Taebaek, South Korea

Image courtesy of the author

they said. "It's called L'Abri." Neither Dean nor his wife was interested in another guru, but they didn't have any pressing need to return. So they went.

They found a hippie commune without a bed to be had; they were offered a mattress on the floor. At breakfast, Dean's wife asked him what he thought. "Another commune, another guru," Dean replied.

Still, they set out on a winding mountain trail to meet the "guru"; as they hiked they met a long-haired, bearded man in mountaineering knickers, who brightened on seeing them. He'd been coming down to meet them, he said. He introduced himself: this was Francis Schaeffer.

L'Abri (Shelter), still operating around the world, is the residential ministry that Francis Schaeffer and his wife, Edith, began in 1955. The idea is relatively simple: A group of people live together, work, study, and pray together; most of the residents are short-term guests dealing with some long-term struggle. The community is open to anyone willing to participate – it is safe to doubt, safe to ask questions, safe to be honest.

But the genius of L'Abri lies in that conversation on the mountainside. Telling the story thirty-five years later, Dean was moved. "I'd never been greeted like that by anyone." There

was nothing smarmy about Schaeffer, he says, nothing fraudulent. There was only a man who found human beings fascinating. He cared about them. So intense was his focus on each person he met that many others report the same feeling of being truly seen for the first time.

The feeling at L'Abri is of coming home; it is the kind of place where a person can be fully seen and fully loved. It is, in other words, a place that encourages people to see one another as God sees them through Christ. For Dean and his wife, who became Christians soon afterward, the greeting was a welcome into the rest of their lives.

Poets in This Issue:

Sally Thomas is a poet, fiction writer, essayist, and teacher. She has taught in both the high school and university classroom, and has served as poet-in-residence in various elementary, middle, and high school settings in the United States and Great Britain. Her most recent book is *Motherland: Poems* (Able Muse, 2020). She lives in North Carolina.

James Crews's work has appeared in *Ploughshares, Raleigh Review,* and the *New Republic,* among other journals, and he is a regular contributor to the *(London) Times Literary Supplement.* His first collection of poetry, *The Book of What Stays* (University of Nebraska Press), won the 2010 Prairie Schooner Book Prize. He lives in Vermont.

We Must Not Stand By

On the Persecution of China's Uighur Muslims

JONATHAN SACKS

Uighurs at a detention center in Xinjiang, China.

Concentrated in the Xinjiang region of China, the Uighurs are an ethnic group distinct from China's majority Han population. Muslims in a state that is militantly atheistic, they have in recent years suffered from increasing persecution. Today, of the approximately 13 million Uighurs, an estimated one million are imprisoned in concentration camps, where they are used as slave labor, starved and otherwise mistreated, and subjected to "reeducation," hours of propaganda each day in which they are required to renounce their beliefs. The crimes for which one can be sent to such camps include wearing a hijab, growing a long beard, being a member of a family that is religiously observant, and having too many children.

China's laws against women having more than two children – three in rural areas – are enforced ruthlessly against Uighur women, who are in many cases forced to undergo abortions and sterilization; as a result, reports the

Rabbi Lord Jonathan Sacks is an international faith leader, philosopher, theologian, and author. He was awarded the Templeton Prize in 2016 and served as the Chief Rabbi of the United Hebrew Congregations of the Commonwealth from 1991 to 2013. RabbiSacks.org @RabbiSacks

Associated Press, birth rates in the mostly Uighur regions of Hotan and Kashgar fell by more than 60 percent between 2016 and 2018. And recently, drone video has surfaced showing Uighurs, bound and heavily guarded, apparently being herded into trains bound for these concentration camps. Confronted with the video on July 19 by BBC journalist Andrew Marr, Chinese Ambassador to the United Kingdom Liu Xiaoming could not explain away what he was seeing. —The Editors

A S A HUMAN BEING who believes in the sanctity of human life, I am deeply troubled by what is happening to the Uighur Muslim population in China. As a Jew, knowing our history, the sight of people shaven-headed, lined up, boarded onto trains, and sent to concentration camps is particularly harrowing. That people in the twenty-first century are being murdered, terrorized, victimized, intimidated, and robbed of their liberties because of the way they worship God is a moral outrage, a political scandal, and a desecration of faith itself.

In 1948, in response to the horrors of the Nazi regime, the nascent United Nations proclaimed the Universal Declaration of Human Rights. China – the Republic of China; the People's Republic (PRC) would not be established until the following year – was a signatory. In 1971, the PRC reaffirmed that commitment, signing the Declaration. Everyone, Article 18 declares,

> has the right to freedom of thought, conscience and religion; this right includes freedom to change his religion or belief, and freedom, either alone or in community with others and in public or private, to manifest his religion or belief in teaching, practice, worship and observance.

The worldwide implementation of Article 18 remains one of the great challenges of our time. This right is too often lost when one group within a society, usually the dominant group, sees another group as a threat to its freedom and its own dominance, or when there is a struggle between the will to power and the will to life. Threat becomes fear, fear becomes hate, and hate becomes dehumanization. The Nazis called Jews vermin and lice. The Hutus of Rwanda called the Tutsis *inyenzi*, or cockroaches. When the world allows the dehumanization of the Other, evil follows, as night follows day.

In both these cases – in the 1930s and in the 1990s – much of the world stood by and watched, paralyzed or indifferent. Yet in both cases, there were also voices of protest with many individuals putting their own lives in danger to protect the lives of others.

Today, that dehumanization is happening to the Uighur population in China. It must be challenged by the global community in the strongest possible terms. Inspired by the courage and actions of men and women who spoke up in the past, we must reaffirm a fundamental truth: that our common humanity precedes our religious differences. Lose this and we lose ourselves and our humanity. We must not allow this to happen. We must not stand by. ⤳

Many detainees' families have been kept in the dark about the fate of their loved ones.

An
Interview
with
Emmanuel
Katongole

Deep Solidarity

The Covid-19 pandemic is a summons to live out new visions of community, says Emmanuel Katongole, a Catholic priest ordained by the Archdiocese of Kampala, Uganda, who teaches at the University of Notre Dame. In June, Jake Meador talked with him about African politics, Christian nonviolence, failing institutions, and how the church should respond.

Jake Meador: Let's get right into a topic you've written about recently: why violence and corruption continue to plague so many countries in Africa. In your book *The Sacrifice of Africa*, you argue that the reason for this is not the failure of the nation-state in Africa, as many assume, but rather its *success*. Could you explain?

Emmanuel Katongole: I wrote the book in part in response to the endless cycles of poverty, violence, and corruption in many parts of Africa, including my own country, Uganda. You often hear about the dysfunctional nature of politics in Africa; you hear about different techniques to help the nation-state become more rational, more transparent, more effective.

But all these proposals assume that African nation-states are the way they are – often with disorder, violence, and poverty – because they're still at an early stage of history. We will, the story goes, eventually progress to a more rationalized, bureaucratized system, able to effectively deliver services and promote the common good. But that is misleading. In order to understand why, one has to do a little bit of archaeology, so to speak: one must dig into the foundational assumptions of the African nation-state, of when, how, and why it came into existence. That is what I try to do in *The Sacrifice of Africa*, which led me to see that the

Father Emmanuel Katongole, PhD, is a core faculty member of the Kroc Institute for International Peace Studies at the University of Notre Dame. He was earlier the founding co-director of the Center for Reconciliation at Duke Divinity School. His most recent book is Born from Lament: On the Theology and Politics of Hope in Africa *(Eerdmans, 2017), and he has just completed another manuscript on issues of identity and violence called* Who Are My People?
Jake Meador is editor-in-chief of the Mere Orthodoxy *blog.*

Artwork by Kasambeko Paul. Used by permission.

Previous spread: artwork by Cliff Kibuuka. Used by permission.

African nation-state is a successor institution to the colonial regime. The latter was set up to benefit, not the colonized peoples of Africa, but rather the colonial centers. Accordingly, whatever "development" was set in place simply represented the minimum required to maintain the colonial system of control and extraction.

At independence, when power was finally wrested out of the hands of the colonial regimes, the African elites became the *de facto* rulers. Yet the institutions they inherited continued to work out of the same imagination of control and extraction. They continued not only to depend on the colonial centers in systems of commerce, but also to serve elite interests. This is what I refer to as "King Leopold's ghost."

So when people say "Africa is dysfunctional," I reply, no, it's not. Given the foundational assumptions – that is, the nation-state – politics in Africa actually works as intended.

Meador: It's done what it's designed to do.

Katongole: Exactly. That is why what is needed is not just recommendations to help democracy flourish or to make the nation-state work better. We need to reimagine politics from a new point of view.

Meador: Your discussion of the Nigerian writer Chinua Achebe's novel *Things Fall Apart* gets at the need to imagine a new political narrative rather than making a nostalgic appeal to something that came before. Can you talk about that?

Katongole: There's a temptation to think, "If only we can recover the precolonial traditions and build from those." Well, yes, this might be helpful. But we must be thoughtful. It is not as if precolonial traditions are standing around

waiting to be recovered. Even if this were the case, there are a number of aspects of precolonial African history and society that I'm not sure I want recovered.

Things Fall Apart was crucial to me in thinking this through. There's violence in the protagonist Okonkwo's village before the coming of the colonialists; many are killed, women are abused. This is not a perfect society.

The book contains a scene in which Okonkwo and the village's traditional leaders confront the colonialists, and Okonkwo kills one of the Europeans. I read this scene as showing two different forms of violence meeting in the marketplace. In a way, it is a picture of what is happening in Africa now. Some precolonial forms of violence come together with new forms of violence, issuing in what I call a unique form of African modernity.

My interest is, how do we move through this? Simply recovering or recreating the past is not the way history works.

Christianity, I think, might provide a way forward. Well, of course I think that – I'm a Christian! But I'm also committed to nonviolence, to the vision of true peace at the heart of the Christian story. If we were to live into that, it might provide us with a way of working

Kasambeko Paul, *Market Day*

Previous spread: Cliff Kibuuka, *Docked at Ggaba 3*

Kasambeko Paul, *Boat Trip*

through the violence at the intersection of precolonial, colonial, and neocolonial forms of violence in modern Africa.

Violence Is Not Inevitable

Meador: You've thought a lot about the question of violence. In the Enlightenment tradition of political theory, violence is assumed to be at the center of the picture. Max Weber, for example, says the state is that entity which has a monopoly on violence; Thomas Hobbes speaks of the pre-political life as fundamentally marked by violence, which must be tamed by a more violent nation-state. One of the things Christianity can do is to remind us that violence is not in fact the natural state.

Katongole: I learned from the theologian John Milbank that what you posit in the beginning as an assumption eventually succeeds in creating the very reality that is imagined. This is the whole point about the political imagination; it's not just a kind of fantasy. Thus, the assumption that violence is the natural order of things, that it's always really what's going on, soon enough becomes a self-fulfilling prophecy: violence becomes an essential part of the political order. And then all one can hope for is to control it, not to completely overcome it. Milbank debunks this assumption that violence is inevitable. I find his argument powerful.

But I also find powerful Milbank's invitation for Christians to rediscover the power of the Christian story. The pathos of modern theology, Milbank says, is its false humility: "We are Christians," we tend to say, "but we are only a religion after all. We have to wait for sociology and political science to provide the 'facts' upon which we can build, to which we can add spiritual truth as a nice gloss." Milbank says that is wrong. What Christians believe about society, about God, about human beings being created in the image of God are *facts*. When Jesus talks about loving our neighbors, and tells us that if we have something against a neighbor, we must come together to reconcile before we bring our gift to the altar, that is basic sociology. Let's not sell ourselves short by saying, "Well, this is just a spiritual principle." We need to reclaim theology's place as queen of the sciences, so that Christian theology *is* sociology.

A Time for Solidarity

Meador: Earlier this week you sent me these words from Cardinal Turkson: "We are rediscovering how much the destiny of each of us is linked to that of others. We are rediscovering the value of the things that matter and the worthlessness of so many things that we once considered important." For a lot of people that point has come as they're making sense of Covid-19; I know you're in Uganda now – what are you seeing in regard to the pandemic?

Katongole: The attention that has been given to Covid-19 here is very impressive, just amazing! Everyone is trying as much as possible to keep it from exploding: the country was locked down for over two months and everyone came on board. But I can't help thinking that if the same leadership and effort were given to the realities that kill people here daily – malaria, diarrhea, malnutrition, poverty itself – we would be a completely different country. Why has that not been the case? I think in some ways it's because realities such as malaria and malnutrition have been accepted as just the way things are in Africa. And as long as these things kill only or mostly

Africans they never get the attention they deserve. One reason Covid-19 has received such a response is that it was killing Europeans and Americans and we thought, "Can you imagine what it's going to do to the Africans?" Why do we wait to hear from WHO before we act? It's part of that problem of imagination. We see it in how we think about economics, too. We wait for the IMF and World Bank to define what Africa needs.

Speaking of economics, Covid-19 has revealed a major vulnerability of development economics in Africa. I have seen such terrible poverty over these months of shutdown in the semi-urban areas and slums. But so much of African politics and economics is centered around the city. It seems to think that nothing of interest happens in villages, which are poor and backward; people become interesting when they move to the city, where "development" happens. Covid-19 has revealed the city as very fragile indeed, and the village as the future.

It still hasn't struck Africa as much as it has struck Europe and America. As a Christian, a theologian, I say, well, maybe this is a time for Our Lady's words in the Magnificat: God brings down the mighty. I think it has revealed vulnerabilities in Western society and America. The systems that we thought worked so well, that we took for granted, made us think that such a disaster could never happen there. Covid-19 has provided a *kairos* moment, a unique opportunity where God intervenes, issuing both an invitation and a challenge. The invitation in the moment is always to live into a new future.

It is a warning, as well. *Kairos* moments are always connected to prophecy; the crucial role of the prophets always is to point to signs of the time. Because when we are going on with our daily work, we may not see them. Prophets also invite the community into lament and repentance, where they may discover something on the other side: hope.

To the extent that we are not drawn into lament, we cannot be drawn into the future. I like especially Jeremiah, who warned the leaders and the prophets and the priests for not healing the wounds of the people – "my people"– rightly. They had said, "peace, peace," when there was no peace. They moved too quickly to "let's get back to normal." That is taking healing lightly.

Think of the lament in Joel, after the locusts came. From the priests, to the kings, to mothers, to babies, everybody put on sackcloth. But after the mourning, "the Spirit of the Lord will be poured upon everyone . . . old men will dream dreams . . . young men will see visions" (Joel 2:28). This only happens in the context of lament. I think after Covid-19 we desperately need new visions of something more than just the old order improved a little. We need new visions of community, of society, and, in America, of a post-racial world. This can only emerge out of a deep practice of lament, of turning to God, of turning to one another in solidarity. Then, your young men and women will see visions and the old men and women will dream dreams of a new future.

We need this desperately. The old world has run its course. You cannot polish things up a little bit and pretend that everything will be okay. That's why I take Covid-19 seriously as a *kairos* moment.

Here in Uganda the lockdown coincided with an extraordinarily powerful rainy season: rivers and lakes flooding, homes destroyed, businesses destroyed. This points to an area in need of urgent attention – it calls us to care for the creation in this new moment. Why haven't we paid the same attention to ecological degradation that we are paying to Covid-19? Covid-19 and the rains are connected.

In America, it is coinciding with racial tensions, frustrations. Don't be too quick to separate them! Both Covid-19 and racism call us to the discipline of lament. And it may, if we turn to God, issue into new visions of a world of justice and interconnectedness, of deep solidarity, a world we share together. This cannot happen when we are so full of ourselves and so full of confidence, when we think that we are an invincible people, a superpower, that we are the best of God's creation. New dreams cannot happen then. I think this is something God is communicating to us in this time.

This is how these things flow into each other. We need solidarity, and not only solidarity with one another, black and white, rich and poor. We need to respond to this *kairos* moment as a crucial moment in the journey into a new future and a new society that is in the process of being born. God is always at work building his new creation. What we are experiencing right now is part of that. This is a very significant time. But this kind of business cannot happen without tears, without blood, without pain.

The Church's Calling

Meador: In *Sacrifice of Africa*, you argue that the church has a central role to play in preserving the good life within a political community. But the sex-abuse scandals in the Roman Catholic Church and in Protestant churches, as well as the scandal of the way that American Evangelicals have rallied around Trump, have caused churches to lose social legitimacy. Is it possible for the church to draw us together and help us remember what is true?

Katongole: The challenge of Africa is a challenge of institutions; I realize that is true of America as well. Institutions that we trusted have been discredited when we most need them.

Artwork by Kasambeko Paul. Used by permission.

The church is called into the world to be its salt. A friend of mine used an image – since it is in the very nature of meat to rot, the crucial question is, "Where was the salt when the meat was rotting?" When you put salt into the meat, the salt disappears. That's the only way it can work. It does not call attention to itself; it is not the thing that is noticed. Rather, the meat is preserved, its flavor enhanced.

Our rotting institutions are concerned about their self-preservation. This must not be the preoccupation of the church. Christians have to be willing, in a sense, to disappear like that salt. We need to go back to the basics, to the sense of Christianity as a story, a story of loving relationship with the world, a saving story, an amazing story. Too often we have nearly lost that excitement. "Were our hearts not burning on the way?" Our churches need a little bit of that. But that requires simplicity and stripping away, as we hear Christ teaching us. One can experience an elemental joy in living very simply.

Pope Francis uses the image of the field hospital. The church is not just for herself. She is a field hospital in the middle of a battle, saving lives. In the middle of battle, with so many wounded, one does not first ask the wounded, "Are you gay? Are you straight? Are you black? Are you from Nebraska? Are you from Texas? Are you from Uganda?" One needs to first attend to the wounds, or bring the wounded to the hospital!

But we have this need to know exactly who is in, who is out, who is going to hell. How did we get to that? So, I think the challenge is, how does Christianity get reimagined? Pope Francis says that we cannot do this if we do not connect with the poor, the weak, the homeless, the most marginalized. The margins are what save us from thinking as slaves of the center. I think that's where Christians can

Kasambeko Paul, *Ship Cruise*

recover a bit of our soul and be light – and salt – for the nations.

Meador: How do you see the Eucharist helping us understand what living well together ought to look like?

Katongole: The Eucharist is the bedrock of Christian memory, and, because memory is a part of the imagination, of the Christian imagination. In the Eucharist, all the elements of the Christian story come together. It proclaims the good news: The new creation is here! The Eucharist draws us into remembering the past, what God has planned, and what he continues to do. It also draws us to remember the future. It reminds us where we are and where the story is headed. It locates us.

Saint Paul says, over and over again, "In Christ God has been reconciling the world." It is through Christ that this reconciliation happens: the Eucharist helps us remember his suffering, death, and resurrection. We remember the institution at the Last Supper, the day before he died: he took the bread and he blessed and broke it and gave it; he took the wine and he blessed it and gave it. And then they ate. That is the memory that shapes the lives of Christians. It is the taking, the giving thanks, the breaking, the giving, the eating,

Kasambeko
Paul,
Tree of Life

and then the sending forth: Go! Do this in memory of me. Go into the world!

I think this is what is unique about the Christian story, shaping lives that are Eucharistic. We must first receive, before we even try to do. That's what I find so frustrating about so many discussions of reconciliation and forgiveness. When I talk to people about forgiveness, they are immediately interested in their agency: "How can I forgive?" they ask. "What are the steps?" I want to say, "Wait a minute, that is not how the story begins." It begins with God's reconciliation, and with us not as the agents but as the recipients of God's reconciliation and forgiveness. The problem is that quite often we don't think there is anything wrong with us. We think the problem is that other guy. But we ourselves

have needed that forgiveness, and it has been given to us, as a gift.

Meador: It's Adam in the garden, "This woman who you gave me – she's the one who did wrong! Not me! I'm fine!"

Katongole: Exactly. And the woman says, "It's the snake! It's not me!" But in the Eucharist we receive everything we need as a gift. And we don't have to pretend any longer that we are not needy, that we did not need that forgiveness, that love. Perhaps what we need to be doing more and more is to draw up examples, stories of people who are living into that forgiveness, as what the church looks like. ⌖

This interview, conducted on June 11, 2020, has been edited for clarity and length.

Photograph by Peter Willi / Bridgeman Images

The Church Is Other People

Why We Need to Gather in Person

NOAH VAN NIEL

ON A BOOKSHELF in my office I have a small replica of *The Cathedral* by Auguste Rodin, bought at the Rodin Museum in Philadelphia when I lived there many years ago. I was taken with its simple beauty: two hands, suspended in time, their fingertips barely touching, forming a gentle arch like the buttresses of a Gothic cathedral. At first glance the statue appears to show hands brought together in prayer, but on closer examination you realize it actually depicts two right hands – what initially presents as a private moment of piety is actually a moment of connection between two individuals. The "cathedral" is contained in the space between two people about to hold hands. Lovers? Strangers? We do not know. All we see is the promise of touch, connection, communion, frozen inches away from realization.

Recently I have had a lot of time to contemplate this statue. It is positioned just over my shoulder in the little Zoom window which

Auguste Rodin, *The Cathedral*, 1908

Noah Van Niel is an Episcopal priest currently serving at The Chapel of the Cross in Chapel Hill, North Carolina, where he lives with his wife and two children. He studied English literature at Harvard College and holds a Master of Divinity degree from Harvard Divinity School.

has been my primary source of connection with my parish these last few months. As I log hours of screen time trying to hold together a congregation – each member confined to his or her own little window – the statue has started to taunt me with everything I am missing and longing for: Touch. Connection. Community.

The hands are not the only reminder of what I long for during this time of pandemic. As I make my way through the New Testament in my daily devotions the moments that speak most loudly are the times when Jesus is with people. He is almost always with people. From the outset of his ministry he recruits disciples to follow him. He brings huge crowds together to teach. He travels with people and enters their houses to eat and stay with them; he gets right up into their faces to touch and heal them; he washes their feet; he puts their children on his knee. Close contact with other human beings, to communicate the presence and power of God, is essential to the movement he founded.

Likewise, as I read Paul's letters, I remember that while he was the church's great founding theologian – making meaning of Jesus' life, death, and resurrection, and speaking of them far and wide – most of his effort was given to forming, nurturing, and sustaining communities of people. For Paul, the keystone of the Christian way was the *ekklesia*, the communal gathering in which one could practice, in the flesh, a way of being together, existing primarily *with* and *for* one another. This gathering was the core unit of the faith, and he spilled much ink trying to keep those disparate units together, for without those bodies, there was no Body of Christ.

This remains the primary work of the church. You learn quickly when you enter the ministry that despite the high talk of heavenly calling, we are primarily in the people business. We spend almost as much time preparing for and attending fellowship events and meetings as we do reading scripture and theology. Our presence at picnic tables and potlucks is as important as our presence at the Eucharistic table on Sunday mornings. This is not a distraction from ministry, but an essential part of it. Christian discipleship was never meant to be an isolated endeavor; it has always meant creation of, participation in, and care for community. One's individual relationship with God is expected to shape how one functions in relationship with others, so facilitating and nurturing real, physical connections between people is a critical function of the church.

This commitment to community is grounded in the doctrine of the Incarnation. An incarnational understanding of the world holds that the wondrous works of God are almost always revealed in and through bodies. "The Word became flesh and dwelt among us." "A virgin shall conceive and bear a son." "Take, eat, this is my body, this is my blood." "Reach out your hand and put it in my side." From Christmas through Easter and across the rest of the liturgical year, the Christian faith is built on corporeal events meant to communicate that God is revealed in the physical realm. When we occupy a common space, there is energy, electricity; a spirit is kindled. It can be felt in the crowd at a sporting event or when sitting silently by the hospital bed of a loved one. Physical presence matters in ways that are impossible to measure but impossible to deny. This is why, in an increasingly fragmented world, the church remains one of the few places whose express intent is to create close contact with other people – because we believe it's good for you, because we believe that God is to be experienced most fully in community and connection. It's why we take great pride in opening our doors to newcomers and old-timers, friends and strangers. To have the banker and the busker rubbing shoulders at the same altar is a sign of glory in our eyes. Because to us the body is a place of divine revelation, and bodies gathered together bring the Spirit of God to life.

All that is missing right now. It's going to be a long time before we're all holding hands again or sharing the same air. This is spiritual starvation as well as social – so long as we must remain physically distant, the church cannot be what it was created to be. Until we can all gather again in person, to eat and sing and pray and work, the Body of Christ is not whole: it is wounded. That is not to say the church cannot be helpful and comforting and do good work in this time. But what people are longing for right now – touch, community, connection – are precisely the things we were made to give them, and cannot.

It is hard to overstate just how frustrating this is to a church leader. And none of the options we're presently offered for proceeding can completely alleviate that frustration. Reopening churches as usual, without any restrictions, gives us the gift of incarnated community but jeopardizes the very bodies we seek to celebrate as revelations of the divine. Saint Paul said to the Corinthians about their communal gatherings, "Now in the following instructions, I do not commend you, because when you come together it is not for the better but for the worse" (1 Cor. 11:17). And if Paul were alive today, I think he would count potentially spreading a disease as infectious and deadly as the coronavirus as "for the worse."

Another option is to open to very small groups of people, none of whom can be at "high risk," and to undertake rigorous screening, distancing, and safety protocols – no singing, no touching, no communion – before we can worship "together." This provides

Until we can all gather again in person, to eat and sing and pray and work, the Body of Christ is not whole: it is wounded.

a minimally satisfying in-person worship experience, serving instead to emphasize current fractures in the community as well as feelings of division and loneliness. Yet another approach is not to reopen at all until the virus is defeated, using instead livestream or recorded services, insisting that the church can keep being the church without the physical gathering that has always been at its heart. So calendars are filled with Zoom calls, Sunday worship is streamed, and meanwhile bodies languish in isolation.

Instead of a satisfying way forward, we are left with a desire that cannot be met. An absence that cannot be filled. A yearning that is perpetual.

But what if that were its own instructive place to dwell? In an age of immediate gratification, we may be used to getting what we need relatively quickly, but in our spiritual tradition, the concept of holy longing is not new. We long for heaven while we are on earth. We long for peace in a world of war. We long for justice in a world that continually frustrates those aims. We long for God yet meet him only sparingly. The great mystical theologians speak at length about the sense of unfulfilled desire at the heart of their prayer life. Gregory of Nyssa holds desire (*eros*) to be the force that continually propels us toward God; Julian of Norwich calls it a "thirst"; Teresa of Ávila calls it the "wound of love," which comes from God and is meant to draw us back to God. And Saint Augustine once wrote, "The whole life of a good Christian is an holy desire," because "by longing, you are made capable. . . . God, by deferring our hope, stretches our desire; by the desiring, stretches the mind; by stretching, makes it more capacious. Let us desire therefore, my brethren, for we shall be filled." In this time of frustration, the perpetual yearning we know so well could be preparing us for something even greater.

Perhaps, as Augustine implies, this prolonged period of unfulfilled desire will widen our hearts, increasing our empathy for those who live in a perpetual state of longing for what is denied them – peace, justice, equality, safety – all those whose deepest needs remain unmet. And perhaps now, having been deprived of people and connection and community for so long, we will appreciate anew how much we depend upon one another for our own flourishing. Maybe not getting to be the church is exactly what the church needs to awaken the sense of longing and desire that will propel us back into communities of faith that feed us in ways we didn't even know we needed, communities that possess a more capacious spirit and a more generous sense of mission.

So long as this virus remains so wildly out of control we are stuck in a state of holy longing. We're frozen, like those two hands in Rodin's *The Cathedral*. Those hands *want* to hold each other, they *want* to come together, but they can't. To be sure, God does not need people to gather in order for God to be active and present in our lives. But God is not the church. The church is other people. That is the essence of the incarnational reality we proclaim: that God was made flesh, and that the work of the Holy Spirit that dwells in each of us is activated and multiplied exponentially when we gather together. For it is only together that we can fully engage in the higher calling to which we have been called – to build up, nurture, and grow communities of faith and show the world what it means to live by the law of love; to shine as a beacon of hope for what our world yet can be. That remains our calling even if we cannot fully live it. For now, and until we are free to be communities in Christ, we must be stretched out in preparation for an even fuller future than we could have imagined before we had to close our doors. That is my holy hope, born from this time of waiting. A hope that allows me to say, with Augustine, "Let us desire, therefore, my brethren, for we shall be filled." ⤳

Two Poems by James Crews

Altars of Attention

Someone has stacked rock cairns
on top of stumps and stone walls
all along the washed-out road
I walk this morning. Each slab
is balanced by the other like one
right action holding space for the next.
But what is the message of these
small towers shored against the
mossy ruins of a country road?
Are they evidence of an effort
solid enough to withstand wind,
lashing rain and the shrapnel
of beer cans tossed from trucks?
I want to kneel and touch each one,
feel how the tip of one stone
fits into the divot of another,
but I don't. Let them be altars
of attention that testify: someone
paused here and cared enough
to build these things for no reason
other than the pleasure of making them.

August Morning

Our minds give off the light
that reveals the connections
linking us one to the other

like the newly risen sun
making visible the dew-
tipped spider webs spun

in the fields last night:
each shining thread drawing
the separate blades of grass

closer together, weaving
a wide patchwork net
which catches everything

that flies into its path. ⤙

AN INTERVIEW WITH JACQUELINE AND EUGENE RIVERS

BLACK LIVES MATTER

....

and the Church

FOLLOWING THE KILLING OF

George Floyd by Minneapolis police and the international movement it sparked, *Plough*'s Peter Mommsen talked to Rev. Eugene F. Rivers III and Dr. Jacqueline C. Rivers about race, solidarity, and how the church should respond. >>

Plough: **You both have been working for decades as Christian leaders in the Dorchester neighborhood in Boston. What have been your thoughts in the weeks since George Floyd's killing on May 25, 2020?**

Jacqueline Rivers: Mostly, I've been thinking about what the response of the church should be; it's been heavy on my heart because the church has not played a clear role. It seems as though the protesting young people, many of whom are not people of faith at all, are coming out in hundreds of thousands, because we, the church, haven't done enough to advance racial justice and so God has placed this responsibility on the shoulders of nonbelievers.

Eugene Rivers: It's important for the church to think more creatively, and to pay much more attention to history. I'm old enough to have seen the riots the night Martin Luther King was assassinated, April 4th, 1968. The rage young people felt then had been growing, as the theater of struggle shifted beyond the deep South to cities like Los Angeles, where the first major riots happened. Today's movement has been building since the death of Trayvon Martin. Right before George Floyd, we had the deaths of Ahmaud Arbery and Breonna Taylor.

And the church, black and white, did not see deeply enough into the nature of the crisis. We have to look in the mirror and ask, "Where were we? How were so many nonbelievers able to exhibit this level of black–white solidarity?"

Jacqueline C. Rivers is the executive director of the Seymour Institute for Black Church and Policy Studies and a lecturer at Harvard University.
Eugene F. Rivers III is the founder and director of the Seymour Institute for Black Church and Policy Studies.

Why has the movement gained such strength this time?

Jacqueline Rivers: Derek Chauvin knelt on George Floyd's neck, apparently for eight minutes and forty-six seconds – a man died three feet from his face. I think that cold-bloodedness has fueled the outrage.

Eugene Rivers: What hasn't helped is the corruption of the national conversation around race in the mainstream media. For example, the *New York Times* has increasingly veered away from classical reportage to this 1619-ish, subjective, self-referential journalism that shrinks from complexity or ambiguity. All the same, George Floyd's shocking death cuts right through that.

As society has become increasingly polarized, the church needs to say: Let's think, let's not get sucked up into rhetoric and emotion. There are legitimate demands for justice. But we've got to respond boldly, within a framework of *agape* love.

Jacqueline Rivers: It's crucial that the change that comes out of this movement is not merely superficial and symbolic but structural. Of course, many of the suggested reforms are obviously good: changing policing strategies, barring chokeholds, demilitarizing law enforcement. But what about more fundamental things like changing police hiring practices? There is a problem of overpolicing, where a minor crime which would go unnoticed in a white neighborhood is immediately pounced upon in a black neighborhood.

Eugene Rivers: The Boston papers are reporting that over five hundred city cops make in excess of $200,000 per year, largely as a result of a bloated overtime system. This creates a perverse incentive: an arrest means court which means overtime for testifying.

Jacqueline Rivers: That's why in some cities where these perverse incentives exist, the slogan "defund the police" may be valid; let's shift spending to where it helps instead of harms. But in other parts of the country, the problem is the opposite. There we may need to pay police *more* generously in order to attract higher quality officers, provide better training, and achieve greater accountability.

You both have been involved in promoting community policing for over two decades. What have you learned?

Jacqueline Rivers: Starting in 1998 we've worked with community activists and law enforcement, local and federal, meeting together weekly on Wednesday mornings to talk over challenges facing the neighborhood. This past Wednesday, we had a conference call to discuss the current unrest, and so many wanted to make clear that we have good cops. In poor black neighborhoods, people *want* to have police. They recognize that not every police officer is Derek Chauvin – that although some structures of policing need to be changed, there are many cops who work for the good of the people.

So the answer is not to abolish the police, as some are calling for?

Jacqueline Rivers: Absolutely not. Because there's another truth that few want to talk about. As horrendous as Derek Chauvin's actions were, the number of young black men who die at the hands of police officers is a tiny fraction of the number who die at the hands of other young black men. We're not often willing to engage that question; it's so much more difficult to respond to. I can decry the racist white cop when it's Derek Chauvin. What do I do when it's my son, or my nephew, or the little boy who grew up next door to me, who is the murderer?

There is structural racism underlying that, too. Hopelessness about jobs, lack of access to high-quality education, and worst of all, residential segregation. Does it matter whether we can or can't live next to white people? Only insofar as city services, quality of education, et cetera, are better where white people live and worse where black people live. So that contributes to a kind of nihilism. How do we expand structural change beyond policing and address some of these larger underlying problems?

You pointed out that Christians have too often been at the periphery of today's movement. Going forward, what answers should the church be offering?

Jacqueline Rivers: The church can give hope. From a purely secular point of view, it is discouraging to realize that despite real accomplishments such as the Civil Rights Act and the Voting Rights Act, the civil rights movement of the 1960s did not eliminate white supremacy.

But we as the church know that in the long run, God is in charge; he's the source of righteousness and justice, and the church will endure. So if we accept our mantle, we can begin to work for the long term, beyond when today's movement has run its course. Whether this movement lasts five years or ten years, we as the church can be the permanent part of the solution.

To do this the church really needs to have a deep understanding of what is going on, to study problems in all their complexity. That means persistence and reading up, not just grabbing the first black person who comes along and saying, "Explain this to me."

And let us break out of our racist segregation in the church and really see how we can work together. Peter, I like the question you asked in an earlier conversation: "What about white people going to black churches?" I think

the expectation about integration is that black people will go to white churches. How radical would it be for white people to go to black churches – and not take over? Too often, that's the expectation.

Eugene Rivers: The church must stay true to itself. Though Christians must stand in solidarity with the protesters, we cannot compromise our fundamental beliefs. At a certain point, for example, I've got to engage the Black Lives Matter organization and their anti-Christian agenda regarding sexuality and gender. Because they're fomenting civil war in the black community with their rejection of the very idea of male and female.

Dr. Jacqueline C. Rivers and Rev. Eugene F. Rivers III

How do Christians stand in solidarity while not aligning ourselves with aspects of the movement with which we cannot agree?

Jacqueline Rivers: It's important to declare what you're *for* – when I went to the protest march here in Boston everybody had a sign. I could carry a sign that makes a Christian statement, a sign that talks about the God of justice. It's not necessarily easy to make clear what you are against in a situation like that, but you can make a strong statement about what you are for. The march I went to was cosponsored by Black Lives Matter and another group, and they opened with what sounded to me like a very Christian prayer. Not everybody who says "Black Lives Matter" is supporting the points of the organization's manifesto that conflict with our faith.

With mainstream culture shifting to an antiracist position, it's of course really tempting to just go with the flow. We need to ask young white protesters: Are you really prepared to deal with what happens when it's time to choose what neighborhood to live in, what kind of school to send your children to? What decisions will you make then? All too often, I think the decisions reflect limited personal or family interest, but they're not the kind of decisions that bring about structural change.

That is why I find it important to start this process by really doing the research and reading – really understanding the nature and the history of white supremacy, learning to appreciate how difficult it is to solve structural problems such as residential segregation. Because only then can we start working toward long-term change.

Eugene, you've written for *Plough* how movements for racial justice are weakened when they ignore the spiritual nature of the struggle. How does that apply now?

Eugene Rivers: Christians need to talk about the real roots of white supremacy. It's not simply oppression and injustice, it's pure evil. Good, spirit-filled Christians are not really prepared to understand the depth of the evil and the sadism associated with this anger.

Jacqueline Rivers: There are "principalities and powers" at work in white racism, to use the words of the apostle Paul (Eph. 6:12). Look at the eerie persistence of white supremacy: it's morphed from slavery to Jim Crow to mass incarceration. Actually putting it to death seems to me beyond human control – we have got to approach it with prayer. That's a thing the church can bring to bear that these radical young white people cannot. They don't understand the true nature of the problem. They don't recognize that the only enduring answer is seeking God's power and relying on him to intervene.

In addition to prayer, the question of unity is also important. If we harbor in our hearts the same racist inclinations that come from white supremacy, we can't really be united in the power of the Spirit to resist it. So it's important for us to work toward that unity between white and black churches. This means white churches taking on the issues that are important to black churches. "Are you working on issues around teenage pregnancy? Are you working on public education?" Maybe you're just struggling to survive as a black church in a gentrifying neighborhood.

Eugene Rivers: I think the church has a unique, singular opportunity in history. And God is kind to us; he gives us these *kairos* moments where if we'll humble ourselves and pray, he will heal the land. He'll do that, but we've got to be willing to pray, seek God's face, humble ourselves.

Jacqueline Rivers: And turn from our wicked ways. We must confront the history of the white church and our complicity in white supremacy. From the period of slavery there has been a component of the church that has not stood up for racial justice. Some of the most powerful proponents of slavery were white clergy who argued for that cruel institution on the grounds of scripture. In fact, the Baptist, Methodist, and Presbyterian churches all split because the Southern congregations were so committed to slaveholding. In the twentieth century there have been some efforts at reconciliation, but many white churches, particularly in the South, have not opposed racial injustice as they ought. Recently there were reports of black Christians leaving white churches because of their support for racist policies. We have to confront this.

Eugene Rivers: We've got to pray. We've got to repent. Then we've got to engage the truth. The churches must understand more clearly that intercessory prayer is an indispensable political resource for struggle. Rev. Martin Luther King Jr., during the most intense periods in the Birmingham and Selma nonviolent campaigns, when confronted by violent police would kneel and pray for his enemies.

We recognize the effects of white supremacy in human hearts and minds, as well as in institutions. But more importantly, we know that God has given us the power to battle and ultimately overcome all principalities and powers through his Son, our Savior.

That means praying like New Testament Christians, so that the power of the Holy Spirit can be poured out as it was at Pentecost. We must discern the principalities and powers we fight against; we must pray against them and teach against them. This is where boldness comes in, right? It takes extraordinary boldness to say, "White supremacy is a demonic spirit. The source of it is pure evil. But the Spirit of the God in Jesus Christ is stronger." ➤

This is a shortened version of an interview by Peter Mommsen on June 19, 2020. Read the full interview at plough.com/blmchurch.

Photograph by DBF... | Milton Spruance... Milton Spruance...

Traveling Inside

The walls of a prison
close off the world;
a stage can open it.

ASHLEY LUCAS

MANY PEOPLE HEAR THE WORD *prisoner* and think *crime*. I hear it and think *father*. My first journey into prison took place when I was fifteen years old – on Christmas Eve 1994, when my mother and I pulled in to a prison parking lot for the first time. My father had been convicted by a Texas court about a month before, plunged into our way down country roads with a paper map spread across the dashboard. At the gatehouse, a guard searched our car and took away our map. We were told that it – on which the prison did not appear, and which would never have left our car – was contraband; it could help someone escape. The officer showed no concern for the fact that we now had nothing

> **I have had to travel to the world's prisons to understand what was happening to my own family, to see the things my father could not show me and to listen to others tell the stories he could not bear to tell.**

the depths of a system we had no idea how to navigate. At that time, the Texas prisons threw new admissions into "diagnostics" – a thirty-day period during which a prisoner can have no contact of any kind with loved ones. We did not even know where he was until he wrote us a letter for the first time. My mother and I immediately flew to the nearest airport and rented a car. (These details point to a degree of economic privilege not shared by many families of the incarcerated. They also point to a truth about how privilege and oppression can not only coexist but cooperate; sometimes you are allowed just enough opportunity to negotiate the terms of your devastation.) My father had no way of knowing we were coming.

Prisons are seldom easy to reach. Because of the size of the great state of Texas, my father was over seven hundred miles from home, over eighty from the nearest airport. This was before GPS and cell phones were common; my mother and I used the map the rental car agency gave us to locate the prison. We found

to guide us back to town. Our map was never returned. This was my first lesson in how to understand a prison: there is no map to guide you through this experience, and even if there were, someone would take it away.

I learned much from my early encounters with the carceral state – the systems, institutions, and social norms that enable and perpetuate an extraordinary level of state policing, supervision, and control in our lives. My father would ultimately spend twenty years and five months in prison, and my mother, sister, and I quickly realized that the forces that held him there had much hold on our lives too. Every resource we had was poured into trying to bring him home, put money on his prison account, pay for the outrageously priced collect phone calls, visit him, let him know that he was loved. I sent him so many letters that my neighborhood mail carrier thanked me for supporting the US Postal Service. We had to learn new ways to survive financially, emotionally, intellectually.

Ashley Lucas is an associate professor at the University of Michigan and former director of the university's Prison Creative Arts Project. She is the author of Prison Theatre and the Global Crisis of Incarceration *(Methuen Drama, 2020). A version of this article appears in her new book.*

My father was incarcerated when I was fifteen; he was released when I was thirty-five. He lived in freedom for five and a half years before he passed away. Though he is no longer inside, some piece of me will always live inside a prison. I know too much that I cannot forget.

OUR FAMILY BEGAN THIS JOURNEY with an overwhelming sense that this should not be happening to us, that somehow fate would rescue us from the clutches of a system that neither understood nor cared about my father as a human being or the circumstances of his conviction. The more people I came to know inside the walls, the more I realized how thoroughly unexceptional we were, how much everyone's humanity and dignity were erased by a system that draws a hard line between those who are free and those who are not.

To go to a prison is to travel to a new destination, even if it sits in the center of the city where you live. Often prisons aren't shown on maps; a blank spot on the page belies the presence of hundreds or thousands of people. Refusal to acknowledge the presence of a building or location on official documents suggests a willful obfuscation of the people and activities that take place inside it.

When you do find a prison, the act of entering displaces you from prior reality. Its landscape, the single-gender environment, the rules of engagement, the uniformed staff and inhabitants, the constriction of movement, the sounds and smells all immediately indicate that you have left the known and entered a new realm – one in which you have little control, whether you have come to live, work, or volunteer. Rachel Marie-Crane Williams, who has spent much time making art with women in an Iowa prison, calls this "traveling inside."

I have had to travel to the world's prisons to understand what was happening to my own family, to see the things my father could not show me and to listen to others tell the stories he could not bear to tell. Often as I sit in cars or airplanes with the landscape rushing past me, I think of the stationary nature of life in prison. While I made my way to distant parts of the globe, my father stayed very still for twenty years. After being bounced around to a series of prisons in the first year, he landed in West Texas, surrounded by barbed wire and fields of cotton. There he did the majority of his time in one prison, going outside the fence just a handful of times to receive medical treatment. The disjuncture between my body being swept away so quickly as to remain airborne while another part of me remained clamped to a fixed point in the red earth of Texas frequently left me feeling disoriented. It was the flip side of Johnny Cash's yearning lines: "Well, I know I had it comin'; I know I can't be free, but those people keep a-movin', and that's what tortures me."

The tension between the fixity of life inside prisons and the vast amount of movement required for those outside to access incarcerated loved ones plagues both families and volunteer programs. The onus of travel – the time, distance, cost, exhaustion, and sometimes humiliation – involved in getting to a prison and inside it always falls on the free person because those inside have no means even to attempt to meet us halfway. Incarcerated people cannot witness all the details of outsiders' struggle to enter prisons, but they imagine it and often feel it keenly. They live in the supreme frustration of disempowerment, without the means to support their children and families or to ease the journeys of the volunteers who come to offer programming.

I started writing detailed accounts of my travels as a way of explaining to my father what I was doing. His physical absence from my daily life felt so enormous and profound that I needed a way to make sure that we would not lose track of each other. For about the first fifteen years of his time inside, the state of Texas allowed each incarcerated person one collect phone call every ninety days. These calls lasted five minutes each and were egregiously expensive – up to five times the cost of free-world long-distance. We mostly refrained from communicating by phone because if some emergency befell him, my father would have no way to tell us if he had already used his allotted call. Since the prison where he spent the majority of those twenty years was an eight-hour drive from our home, my mother and I could only manage to visit once a month while I was in high school. I saw him just three times a year after I left the state for college.

So we had no choice but to live our family life in letters. My need for my father was so great that I wrote him every day the mail went out. He wrote me about twice a week, and in this manner, we shared more with one another than many people who live in the same home. My many travels to prisons around the world became a way for me to try to better under-stand what surrounded that visiting room in the West Texas cotton patch – the only place where I could put my family back together.

THE FIRST PERFORMANCE I SAW inside a prison caught me off-guard. I had trav-eled to the Louisiana State Penitentiary, popularly known as Angola, to attend an event called Longtermers' Day in 2004. This celebration honored the lives of men who had served twenty-five years or more in prison, and families and visitors were invited to spend the day in the visiting area with over two hundred men. I was twenty-five years old; every man around me, it occurred to me as I looked around the room, had been in prison at least as long as I had been alive.

I had reached out to several staff writers at the *Angolite*, Angola's prison news magazine – I was beginning to write a play about people who have loved ones in prison and I wrote asking about their relationships with their family members. They, in turn, invited me to visit for this event where family members could come inside the walls to spend several hours with their incarcerated fathers, sons, and husbands. Angola has a wide variety of organizations run by incarcerated men, and Longtermers' Day had been put together by the Human Relations Club, a group whose mission is to care for the indigent and elderly and to bury in the prison cemetery those whose families cannot or will not claim their bodies.

Though all the longtermers had been told they could invite their loved ones to the event, I was among fewer than a dozen visitors that year and not related to anyone in the room. Many families could not make the journey to Angola, which sits in a Louisiana swamp over an hour's drive from Baton Rouge. Other longtermers had lost touch with their loved ones or outlived everyone they had known in the free world.

I spent the whole day inside the prison, chatting with the men and listening to several prison bands play. At one point, as we ate heaping plates of jambalaya, two men stood up and started yelling greetings to one another across the tables. The rest of us soon fell quiet as these men claimed the front of the room as a stage and started a performance. Most folks around me knew what I did not – that the players before us were members of the Angola Drama Club. The scene that ensued involved two men standing on a street corner talking

Photograph by Levi Stroud. Used by permission.

about the women they saw walking past them. They had plenty to say, and though the women they described were never seen by the audience, the actors' reactions told the story.

The scene was charming; the audience laughed so much and so loudly that I could hardly hear the dialogue, despite being seated close to the performers. The climax of the play arrived when a third actor – by far the largest man in the room – emerged from the back of the audience dressed in drag, with a messy wig and a giant flowered dress. He lumbered through the audience swaying his hips, and when he reached the main characters, they lost all their fast talk and could not speak to the one "woman" who actually talked back to them.

A group of men in the audience laughed so hard they actually fell out of their seats. Years later, when I started doing programming in other US prisons, I was cautioned at volunteer training never to lead a theater exercise that involved participants lying on the floor, particularly in a group – it could be seen as a security threat, or suggest that someone had been attacked. I have no memory of prison staff being at Longtermers' Day, but they must have been present given the fact that outside visitors were mixed into the crowd. No one objected to the men laughing on the floor. Thus, though I

did not know it at the time, I had watched an act of theater shift the boundaries of what was acceptable or alarming in a prison context.

But then everything about my experience at Longtermers' Day seemed to alter, erode, or entirely undo a boundary of some kind. All that I witnessed that day stood in stark contrast to what I had read and been told about Angola – the grim accounts of the Angola Three, who had each served more than a quarter century in solitary confinement, the stories about men in the general population who slept with phone books on their chests in case someone tried to stab them in the night. The men I met at Angola treated me with great dignity and respect. They took care of one another. The Human Relations Club had spent a whole year organizing this event to honor the fortitude and endurance of those who could survive decades of incarceration, and they celebrated with performances that required considerable talent and skill. Every piece of Longtermers' Day had been rehearsed and curated to ensure that those men and their guests could experience a few hours of distraction – a kind of reprieve from the extraordinary stress, boredom, and indignity of daily life in prison.

Prisoners at a men's penitentiary in Rio de Janeiro, Brazil, watch a performance by the author.

FOR YEARS AFTERWARD, I FOUND I did not have the ability to make my friends and colleagues understand what Longtermers' Day meant to me. How could I explain to anyone in the free world that I had seen some of the best comedy of my life inside one of the most notorious prisons in the United States? How could I convey to others many had never seen a play performed outside. Some had never seen a play until they performed in one themselves as part of a theater program inside the walls.

Most of the people I met wanted to talk about what the theater was doing in their lives at present, how it helped them survive the daily torments of confinement. I realized in listening

> **The play gave us all permission to share a kind of communal joy that is antithetical to the environment of the prison itself.**

the fullness of such happiness and fun inside the same facility that holds Louisiana's death row? What are the ethics of attempting to tell such a story to people in the free world? How could I convince people to have discussions about these kinds of events instead of the crime stories that others often demand to the exclusion of any other narrative about people in prison? The play by the Angola Drama Club gave us all permission to share a kind of communal joy that is antithetical to the environment of the prison itself. Something was going on there that I had never seen before; the practice of theater made the prison into a different kind of space, one that relaxed and united the gathered people, rather than enclosing and isolating them.

In the years my father spent in prison, I became a playwright and theater scholar and discovered that people were making theater in prisons all over the world. I set out to meet, observe, and collaborate with as many of those folks as I could, because I wanted to find out why the theater was meaningful to people living in prisons. The vast majority of incarcerated women and men I met in the course of my research had little to no relationship to theater prior to their imprisonment;

to them that people in prison are often using theater as a strategy to accomplish something else. Many held themselves to high artistic standards and sought to achieve the utmost level of skill they could in rehearsals and performances, but what they gained in doing so transformed their experiences of life inside the walls. Incarcerated actors, stage managers, technicians, and audiences experience the theater as a way to temporarily shift the power dynamics of the prison and to celebrate their life and experience.

Performances inside the walls make the struggles of incarcerated people visible to one another, prison staff, and other audiences. They reveal the ways in which incarcerated people have greater complexity and depth than stereotypes suggest, and can make us question whether any person deserves what the incarcerated endure and whether it makes us safer. Most people do not feel safe when the state has total control of their lives – no one feels safe in prison. Likewise, people in the free world are not safe if the state cannot be trusted to treat all of its residents as full human beings. We should never forget that our notions of freedom are built upon the backs of those who are not free. In the theater we can join together – from both sides of the walls – to imagine a different way to live. ➤

The Solidarity of Grief

EMMA MEIER

I NEVER FELT MUCH PATIENCE for parents who worry a lot about their children. To me, such parents seemed paranoid, always waiting for the phone to ring with some terrible news. Although my six children had their scrapes and tumbles, they always landed on their feet. I trusted their good sense, and Providence. Accidents, illnesses, misfortunes – such things happened to other families, never to mine. So when one day the phone did ring, I was unprepared.

It was one of those beautiful November days when nature turns on its summer charm one last time. My husband, Felix, and I had driven six hours upstate to attend our youngest son's cross-country meet. After a successful race,

---

Emma Meier and her husband, Felix, live at the Mount Community, a Bruderhof in Esopus, New York.

we continued on to Potsdam, New York, to visit our two daughters studying at the Crane School of Music, and to spend the night at the house where they stayed with friends. After enjoying the dinner our girls had prepared, we relaxed in the sitting room. Outside, a clear blue sky turned rosy and darkened – the end of a perfect day.

And then my husband's phone rang.

~

JUST A FEW WEEKS EARLIER, on a similarly beautiful evening, he and I had been enjoying bourbon on the deck when I turned to him and said, "This is so perfect it seems almost like something's missing."

"That's a strange thing to say," he'd replied, "but I think I know what you mean."

Over the previous months, a restless feeling had been growing in me. It was now thirty years since we'd gotten married at the Bruderhof, the community we belong to where Felix serves as a pastor, and it seemed we had everything we'd ever wanted. Our children were healthy, popular, bursting with talents. They were mostly grown or in college; our oldest son had married and already we had our first grandson. It seemed to me we had lived an enchanted life. Was it luck? A blessing? Or had trouble just passed us over? In the vaguest of ways, I felt incomplete. In the course of Felix's ministry, we had counseled many people both within the community and outside it, notably during the two years we'd served in London's impoverished East End. Countless times we had met people bereaved and broken under the wheel of life. Always we had tried our best to console, but to me our words had often seemed like hollow platitudes. My well-intentioned succor grated even on my own ears.

"Felix," I had mused, "our marriage has been so blessed. We have never had to deal with real hardship. Do you think God might ask more of us?"

~

NOW, AS WE ENJOYED another perfect evening, Felix pulled out his phone. The caller was unidentified. "Joe's bed and breakfast," he joked. We all laughed. Then his face suddenly tensed. "Can you repeat that?" he said.

Felix beckoned me over and we strained to catch the caller's words. It was something about Rudi, our second-to-youngest son, our nineteen-year-old, who had so enthusiastically left us six months before to teach English to indigenous children in Paraguay. We heard only snatches. Rudi had had an accident – fallen from a cliff – hospitalized – in a coma – critical condition.

Suddenly the glowing autumn sky turned cold as ice. My skin crawled and my head began to spin. Every thought but the worry for our son vanished from our minds. We sped home, and booked the first flight we could get to Asunción, Paraguay.

All along the way, a brutal kaleidoscope of images assailed me. But through them all, I kept seeing Rudi's face with his slightly crooked grin. He had always been the least demanding of our children: sunny and contented, with a mind full of projects he had schemed up. I saw him standing in the middle of the living room, trailing muddy footprints, proudly smiling over two bunches of radishes freshly harvested from his "organic garden" under the fire escape. I saw him sitting on his bed, wrestling with the rubber strapping of his latest catapult. I saw him surrounded by the little odds and ends he treasured as a child: the chess pieces under the bed; the stray stamps on his desk, leaked from his album; the scraps of metal he'd picked up, awaiting rehabilitation in his homemade forge; his notebooks on the dresser, on the nightstand, under the nightstand – notebooks containing bits of poetry, half-finished short stories, jokes, diary entries.

I saw him as a teenager – gangling, overgrown, with that irrepressible grin. Unlike my other children, he had never developed a drive for competition. I had wanted him to play high school sports, and encouraged him to try out for soccer. Happily, he had set off for the tryouts and returned just as happy to announce he had failed to make the team. "Coach made us run laps around the field," he explained, "but one of the guys couldn't keep up, so I dropped back to run with him. I guess coach wasn't impressed."

I pictured the many little gifts he had made for me over the years: the plant hangers and noteholders he had fashioned from scrap iron, a beautiful filigree bracelet cunningly woven from welding wire.

I pictured the last time I saw him. He had been living with friends, working a job some distance from home. Unexpectedly, he burst into our living room one evening announcing, "I'm off! I'm leaving for Paraguay tomorrow!" He was ecstatic. We knew Rudi had volunteered to teach in a school for indigenous children in the Chaco, so we felt excited for him.

Now, as I sat on the airplane with my head full of Rudi's face but unable to picture the Rudi I was about to see, I opened a notebook of his that I had stuffed in my handbag. In his unmistakable, scratchy handwriting, the poem on the page was titled "Graduation," written just before he completed high school and left home.

You fortunate flower on windowsill
Protected from the storm and wind
Exempt from hardship, grief and thrill,
Never tempted, never sinned.
You gaze with scorn from lofty chair
At kinsmen romping far below,
An emperor, a millionaire:

Immune to predator and foe.
One day you'll grow out of your plastics
And find yourself in natural dirt,
Unshielded by the house of matchsticks,
Find things that heal as well as hurt.
And between the mundane,
You'll find joy requires pain.

~

ARRIVING IN ASUNCIÓN was like walking into a sauna. Not only the heat but the foreign culture and unknown language disoriented us. A friend of Rudi's took us to the hospital and told

Top: Ten-year-old Rudi, project in hand.

Bottom: Can't believe he took the bait! Rudi *(front center).*

Rudi with friends in Paraguay

us what had happened. Rudi had fallen fifteen meters (about fifty feet) while free climbing a sheer cliff. He had been driven in the back of a pickup truck for two hours in extreme agony until he reached the hospital where doctors placed him in a medically induced coma.

When we got to the hospital, I braced myself, but no amount of bracing could have prepared me for the sight of Rudi's broken body shrouded with braces and casts and a tangle of wires and tubes. His chest heaved up and down mechanically, prompted by the ventilator. I felt numb. Shattered. How could this be happening?

But my optimistic reasoning kicked in. Rudi was the toughest of the family, I told myself, the one who never complained. Tall, strong, handsome – he had always exuded enthusiasm for life. If anyone in our family could survive this, it would be Rudi. He would fight like a tiger. But so far from our familiar world, we felt utterly helpless.

~

IN OUR DISTRESS, our community back home supported us. They contacted our insurance company and arranged for Rudi to be medically evacuated to the United States. After

several setbacks, a transfer date was set. Through a translator, Felix and I had understood from the Paraguayan doctors that Rudi's chances of survival were good. Our hope and confidence soared. Surely, once we had Rudi back in the United States, all would be well.

I kissed Rudi's forehead – the only place not covered by medical paraphernalia – before we were ushered away, and the medics began preparing Rudi for his dangerous journey.

After each leg of the flight, text messages from the attending nurse on the jet informed us that all was well. The flight landed safely in Albany, New York, and the surgeons made immediate plans to recall him from the coma before beginning a series of reconstructive operations.

Felix and I had planned to follow by commercial airline, but a violent thunderstorm caused our flight to be canceled. After excruciating delays, we caught another flight and landed at JFK three days later, in a snowstorm. We exited our plane and lined up for the customs inspection. While we stood, squeezed shoulder-to-shoulder with strangers, customs officials barking orders, Felix's cellphone buzzed. A text from our family doctor read, "Call immediately."

My heart fluttered. Instantly, I felt that gut-twisting premonition – here was terrible news. But again I braced myself. Maybe there was just a question regarding the surgery . . . The airport crowd chattered around us, the din punctuated by booming announcements from the intercom. Should we call here, or wait until we have space to talk with more privacy? Felix hesitated, then dialed.

Our doctor's voice, usually calm and genial, was tense and clipped. "Come as quickly as possible," he said. "Rudi's condition is extremely critical." We were stunned. It had to be a mistake. The doctors in Paraguay had said he had been doing well. We fired off questions. We learned that a sudden fluid shift had just ended all brain activity. The doctors in Albany did not expect him to survive more than a few hours.

We stood in the middle of the turmoil in a daze. We passed through customs and stumbled toward baggage claim. The belt had jammed; frustrated travelers stood around impatiently. What was the point of baggage, anyway? Our son was dying. We considered abandoning it. Just then the belt revved back up, and spat out all four of our cases in quick succession. We loaded them on a trolley and flagged down the limousine. With the driver's garrulous chatter, the four-hour drive felt like an eternity.

Finally, walking into the ICU in Albany, we saw our son. In that first moment, I felt that Rudi's soul was no longer with us; he was already in another world. His soul, still bursting with life and energy, had cast off this crippled, broken body and moved on. He was flying free. I sensed him nudging me, smiling, as if to say, "Don't be sad, my work here is finished."

That evening our whole family gathered around his bed. Rudi's older brother Allan led our singing with his guitar, filling in when sobs drowned the melody. The box of tissues was empty. All that night, Rudi's three brothers stayed with him – their last chance to hang out together. They reminisced, sang Rudi's favorite songs, washed his hair, and shaved his chin.

The next morning we gathered again to remove the ventilator. It was 10:24 a.m., December 4.

~

AFTER THE FUNERAL, the days crawled past in a haze. I felt weak and empty. All the certainties of my old life evaporated. If a fluke accident could rob me of my son, then life was built on a butterfly's wing.

Into this lonely void poured hundreds of emails, cards, and text messages from Rudi's friends and classmates all over the world. They told me about a side of Rudi I had scarcely realized. One classmate wrote, "He was probably the only guy I knew in high school who completely disregarded what it meant to be a 'cool guy' and focused on reaching out to those who were sidelined and lonely." A young woman wrote, "Rudi reached out to everyone, but I felt like he especially reached out to me. I hated high school. It was tough accepting who I was and finding my place, and I think Rudi knew that. One time he met me in the hall and said I should join gospel choir because he thought I should do a particular solo. He told me that he liked my voice and thought that I was perfect for the part. Wow! That carried me through a couple of weeks."

The memories that poured in all shared a common theme: Rudi our son, so impulsive and often confounding, had been seeking an authentic life free from hypocrisy and false values – a life lived not for himself, but for others. As we grew to know this side of our son, the magnitude of our loss also grew. But with it came a sense that in some way, short as it was, Rudi had lived a complete life, that he had fulfilled his purpose. Perhaps Rudi himself expressed our feeling best in the final stanza of the last poem he ever sent me:

> Whenever one man's life transcends
> This evil world and stands apart
> No matter how he meets his end,
> It cuts a gash in Satan's heart.

But even with this assurance born of faith, grief overwhelmed us. We watched our friends carry on with busy life, absorbed in the minutiae of daily tasks; but for us, nothing of our former lives seemed to have significance anymore. Every day seemed like an empty chasm we had

to cross. Christmas was only days away. The celebrations, the cheery good humor and jollity that are the hallmarks of the holiday season, jarred our wounded souls. How would we survive it?

In that moment came a call from a father of teenaged children who had recently lost his wife to cancer. He invited us to join his family for Christmas dinner. Although we hardly knew them, we accepted, and instantly meshed. We spent six hours together, sharing pictures and relating memories, crying and laughing. Our shared grief brought us together, connecting us in a way we had never connected with others before. As the evening ended, the conversation lapsed into a comfortable silence. For several minutes, we gazed out the large picture window at the setting sun that sent a cascade of golden light across the Hudson Valley. Unspoken was the knowledge that our loved ones were alive in eternity, awaiting a future reunion.

Some days later, an older couple whose twenty-two-year-old son had died of cancer came to grieve with us. Shortly after that, a middle-aged woman who had found her sister after she committed suicide came to tell her story, then a young couple whose infant son had died hours after birth. In each encounter, we wept and laughed together, our shared grief bridging all barriers.

~

JESUS SAID, "BLESSED ARE THOSE who mourn" (Matt 5:4). I have often puzzled over this Beatitude: how can mourning be a blessing? Now, through Rudi's death, hard as it is to admit, I can say that the mourning we do every day is a blessing. It has bonded us with so many others. Already in the hospital in Asunción, strangers with whom we could not even speak sat and wept with us. They saw our weakness and our woundedness, and responded from their own wounded hearts. We never learned what pain they carried; we only knew they did and understood ours.

The vague feeling of incompleteness I felt before Rudi died has left me. It is hard to explain how a loss can make one complete, but Rudi left me a clue with the last words of his poem, "joy requires pain."

Perhaps he had understood at eighteen something I am learning only now. Since his death, it has dawned on me that Jesus is here, at the bottom of society, among all those who hurt. I have learned that our pain softens the shell that insulates us from the suffering of others. Our grief allows us to absorb their grief, making us a part of the collective suffering of the world, a suffering known and borne by God himself. In this deepest and most profound connection with others, I have found joy. ⤳

Two Sonnets by Sally Thomas

In the Fullness of Time

Time, the hermit thinks, is always full.
Unlike the moon, it does not wax and wane,
But incubates the future endlessly.
It fares forth daily, with its pregnant waddle,
Plods the same road, points the same direction,
Never arrives or labors, or else incessantly
Arrives, every second is giving birth.
The hermit wonders how to understand
This strange phrase from the Gospel writer's hand.
He thinks: Does time itself in time bring forth
Eternity, to intervene in time? –
His head hurts now. The candle's burning low
And won't restore itself. Outside, new snow
Shines. The moon, unveiled, is full in time.

Michaelmas

These autumn afternoons, black thundershowers
Break above the ridge, to rinse the dust
From the slanting light. The last pale tattered coneflowers
Mourn at the hermit's door. Before first frost,
The rain makes everything intense with life.
Today he sees a doe and half-grown fawn
Browsing his ruined garden. In one brief
Glimpse the world holds still. They dapple and darken
On his vision, are more present to him than his skin.
His heart's lost to them. Charged, electric,
The world's more real than human minds imagine.
Its pure unseen intelligences shock
Him into knowing more than he can know.
The deer depart. He does not see them go. ➢

Dinotopian Visions

An Interview with
James Gurney

James Gurney is a neighbor to the Bruderhof community in Platte Clove, New York. He's also the beloved author and illustrator of the book Dinotopia *and its sequels. For this issue,* Plough *editor Susannah Black asked him about his work and the world that he's invented – a place where not only humans of many ethnicities and cultures work together in harmony, but even humans and dinosaurs live in solidarity.*

Plough: The society you portray in your Dinotopia books has, obviously, captivated a huge audience. What about it do you think has been so compelling? What about that world, that alternate social reality, is compelling to you?

James Gurney: What people tell me most often is that they like the sense of immersion they feel when they read the book. Some of that comes from its being an illustrated book, which sketches out so many dimensions of an alternate universe. The reader's imagination adds at least 50 percent to that act of conjuring, filling in the spaces between the pictures and the words. What I find compelling is trying to make the impossible seem inevitable, whether it's a city built on a waterfall or a dinosaur philosopher.

One striking thing about the world you create is its relationship to technology. It is in no sense a primitive society: they have diving machines, hot air balloons, etc. But they also seem to be selective in what they adopt and are drawn to. What is the nature of the Dinotopian approach to appropriate technology?

As the son, grandson, and great-grandson of tinkerers, engineers, and inventors, I've always been fascinated by technology. In particular, I'm interested in how every obvious benefit of a new technological invention is counterbalanced by an invisible cost or compromise that may take a generation or two to recognize. There are so many examples. Even the invention of writing undercut the "palaces of memory" that preliterate societies once had. If there was a period when we might have really taken stock and considered the future more judiciously, it would have been at the advent of electricity, mass production, automobiles, airplanes, and modern communications: in other words, about one hundred and fifty years ago. It's still recent enough and familiar enough to relate to, but it puts our modern dilemmas in some context. We're at a similar crossroads now with the advent of robotics and AI, and I think living intentionally with technology will become even more important.

I created the prequel *Dinotopia: First Flight* to explore those questions from a dystopian point of view. I love the idea of a utopian world that arrived at that place after having survived earlier times of struggle and suffering.

In a similar way, Dinotopia is an urban world, but has many characteristics that I associate with the rural: integration, beauty, balance.

Tell me about how you've chosen to portray cities in these books.

I think those qualities of integration, beauty, and balance can exist in urban worlds as well as rural ones, especially if you start by doing away with cars. I tried to include in Dinotopia everything from crowded urban life to small towns to remote and wild environments. The design of the cities is inspired by the medieval urban design of Old World cities, with their organic street grids and vernacular architecture, rather than the top-down design of more highly professionalized societies. I was also inspired by exposition architecture, such as the 1893 Chicago Exposition, which was a temporary expression of the highest ideals of the American Renaissance.

Tolkien described the imaginative work that artists, and particularly fantasy artists, do as "subcreation": his idea was that we create because we are creatures of a creative God who has made us in his image. Does this idea have resonance with you?

I hadn't read that idea about Tolkien. My understanding (and I may be wrong) was that he saw himself not so much as a creator or a subcreator but rather as a kind of lowly transcriber of some ancient text that already existed.

Thinking this way allows the author to take himself or herself out of the position of creator. That relieves one of the burden of playing God. If you believe your fantasy world already exists, it makes the ideas come more readily to the imagination.

The sense that one gets about the world that you've made is that you love it: you don't just love the characters, but the place itself. Can you talk about that love? What is it like to love something you've made?

Yes, I love the characters with all their flaws and I love the place with all its history. I once printed some travel tickets to Dinotopia that I give to people. The only problem, I tell them, is that they're one-way tickets. My publishing mentor Ian Ballantine, who published Tolkien and a lot of imaginative fiction, was adamant that the purpose of fantasy literature is not to escape, but to engage. It's fun to involve my imagination with a place that doesn't exist, because it makes me appreciate our own world even more.

There is conflict in Dinotopia, but it is a utopia; it's a place where harmony reigns. What is the nature of that harmony? What does the kind of interesting, non-passive, daring peace you've presented there mean to you?

That was an old Turkish maxim that I found somewhere. I needed a saying that started with a "W," so that, reading down all the initial letters of the lines in the Code of Dinotopia, you could read the additional maxim "SOW GOOD SEED." I like the Turkish proverb for the way it upends so many assumptions on various levels. I've always been inspired by the nonviolent examples of Martin Luther King Jr., the Dalai Lama, Gandhi, and of course Jesus. But I focused on that maxim more as a reaction to the militarization of fantasy and science fiction in so many fantasy worlds that I had grown up with, including *Star Wars* and *Lord of the Rings*. The endless battles became, frankly, too predictable and boring. I found it to be much fresher and more difficult to envision a world that had figured out how to live peacefully.

When I was researching post-Darwinian nineteenth-century travel journals, I was struck by the view of the natural world that early explorers came back with, especially from Africa. Gorillas, whales, and even elephants were routinely called monsters and beasts. The more we get to know them, the more we discover how compassionate and sophisticated they are. Dinosaurs were and are ready for such an imaginative transformation. Some of that comes from the science – Jack Horner and other paleontologists discovered how parent dinosaurs took care of their young in nests. We humans are discovering that we can learn something from animals around us. Dinosaurs are my vehicle for that journey of discovering the harmony of nature. I have noticed that earlier nature writers like Alexander von Humboldt often speak of harmony, so maybe we're returning to that.

The Code of Dinotopia holds that "Weapons are enemies, even to their owners." Can you talk about this explicit pacifism? Is that a code you share?

Dinotopia is, among other things, a separatist society: Dinotopians know what's going on outside but choose not to be in contact with the outside world. Have you considered the ethics of Dinotopian separatism?

I hadn't thought of Dinotopia as being deliberately separatist so much as having developed within an impassible region of storms and reefs. I didn't want to deal with trade and colonialism and invasion and other sorts of mass-culture contact. I just wanted to have occasional individual shipwrecked arrivals. The inspiration is from reading James Hilton's

Lost Horizon and Heinrich Harrer's *Seven Years in Tibet*. I am still fascinated by societies that are cut off from the busy interconnected world, societies such as the inhabitants of North Sentinel Island, who to this day have had only fleeting contact with the outside world. What do they make of jet flyovers and ships and plastic bottles? What did the ancient Maya know that we have since forgotten?

Dinotopia is, above all things, perhaps, civilized. That contrasts with the incivility of some characters, and of other societies either portrayed or implied. What does "civilization" mean to you?

Well, to me, "civilization" means the Greek ideals associated with being a member of a city. When I was working as an illustrator for *National Geographic*, I was inspired by research trips to Rome, Athens, and Jerusalem, where I could witness the physical record of how people collectively contributed to something greater and more lasting than the individual can accomplish.

The vision the books seem to conjure up is one of beauty and strangeness and adventure and harmony, both ecological and social, all at once. What would it mean to be inspired by these books to live in a different way in our world?

I'm always amazed by how people of so many different ideological perspectives have embraced Dinotopia, from fundamentalist Christians to evolutionary biologists, from socialists to old-school capitalists. That may be because I largely dodged questions of politics, religion, and economics in the books, and focused instead on pragmatic issues. I didn't have a political or religious message driving the story. Instead the characters (with all their flaws) and the adventure are the focus of the story. I don't have a moral to the story. People hopefully are inspired in various directions, and that's as it should be. ➤

SISTER DOMINIC MARY HEATH

Solidarity
Means Giving Yourself

Can a cloistered nun help a hurting world?

All images courtesy of Anne Goetze

"

AM FEELING CONFUSED RIGHT now about what I want to give my neighbor." A letter from a friend captured the feelings of many Americans this spring. This was back when "the Head Cheetah" – the only name I've heard her use for President Donald Trump that could also be called a term of endearment – sent out relief checks. My friend wanted to give hers away; her husband wanted to keep it against an uncertain future. Meanwhile, she worried that they were falling short in love of neighbor by "aggressive self-focus."

"It's funny I'm telling you this, of all people," her letter concluded, "since I believe you've dropped out of society more than my husband has."

I often hear comments like this about my cloistered life in a Dominican monastery. As a contemplative nun, my days are spent away from mainstream society – no commute, no trips to the grocery, no family vacations. And yet, hard as it is for some to understand, as a nun I do have a vocation to fulfill in solidarity with a hurting world.

In the tradition of Catholic social teaching, solidarity is a modern word but not a new concept. Building on the natural law tradition of great thinkers like Augustine and Aquinas, popes in the twentieth century spoke increasingly of the need for "friendship," "social charity," and a "civilization of love." It was Pope Saint John Paul II, survivor of both Nazi terror and Communist oppression in his native Poland, who began preaching this doctrine with urgency for the new millennium.

"Solidarity," he wrote in his 1987 encyclical, *On Social Concern*, "is not a feeling of vague compassion or shallow distress at the misfortunes of so many people, both near and far.

On the contrary, it is a firm and persevering determination to commit oneself to the common good; that is to say to the good of all and of each individual, because we are all really responsible for all."

We are *all* really responsible *for all*. What does this mean?

N EVERYDAY SPEECH, "SOLIDARITY" can stand for anything from friendly feelings to support for a favorite cause. Standing *with* and standing *for*, that's solidarity, right?

Not exactly. As John Paul II points out, solidarity is not an emotion. Those experiences people have on social media – little bursts of righteous indignation, warm feelings of like-mindedness, the rewarding sense they've done their part by clicking "like" or "share" – nope, not solidarity.

Nor does solidarity mean championing just any cause. According to John Paul II's definition, solidarity is a commitment to an objective standard called the common good. The common good isn't the sum of individual interests, as though the greatest number of students getting their way were the greatest good for the classroom; it's the ideal good for society as a whole, the sum total of social conditions allowing all people to reach fulfillment. Although it doesn't bow to individual interests, the common good is thus very much concerned with the flourishing of individuals: "the good of all and of each."

Opposite:
Anne Goetze,
Bird in Hand

We are all really responsible for all. What does this mean?

Sister Dominic Mary Heath, OP, is a Dominican nun at Our Lady of Grace Monastery, North Guilford, Connecticut.

Cultivating solidarity requires something more of us than warm feelings or unquestioning allegiance. As John Paul II puts it, solidarity means a choice for "the good of one's neighbor with the readiness, in the Gospel sense, to 'lose oneself' for the sake of the other instead of exploiting him, and to 'serve him' instead of oppressing him for one's own advantage." Solidarity, in this deeper sense, draws on our human capacity for making the free and sincere gift of ourselves to others. It is the conviction, carried out in action, that I am my brother's keeper and he is mine; what it asks me to give my brother is nothing less than myself.

> **It is through the free gift of self that man truly finds himself.**

Solidarity is thus concerned with persons, not abstractions. It looks for the needs of the people I live, work, and pray with, beginning in the natural place of self-giving between persons "with the mutual support of husband and wife and the care which the different generations give to one another." When it turns its attention to social policies and public institutions, it judges their health by the good of the persons they serve, especially the poorest and most vulnerable.

The opposite of solidarity, John Paul II tells us, is shrinking into ourselves: "Man is alienated if he refuses to transcend himself and to live the experience of self-giving and of the formation of an authentic human community oriented toward his final destiny, which is God." To refuse solidarity to others by "dropping out" of society – even as a cloistered nun – produces a radical departure from human happiness: "It is through the free gift of self that man truly finds himself."

I LIVE IN A CLOISTERED MONASTERY where some twenty women, consecrated to God by spousal vows, spend our lives in service of the divine liturgy, the public praise of God. Separation from society is of the essence of monastic life. As a nun, I can vote in elections and be called for jury duty, but that's a pretty thin description of the duties inherent in a commitment to the common good. (But do I wear my *I Voted* sticker in the enclosure? Absolutely, I do.)

To understand what solidarity means in the cloister, you have to realize that the self-gift of solidarity is always response to truth. "Man cannot give himself to a purely human plan for reality, to an abstract ideal or to a false utopia," says John Paul II. Monastic life is not one lifestyle choice among others. It is a public statement about the truth of who God is and what human existence means. It says in living words that *this world is not enough*.

All of us in our own vocations need just reasons for serving others when instead we could use, exploit, or ignore them. Three reasons stand out – the dignity of the human person, the reality of sin, and the meaning of redemption.

First, solidarity can only grow from truth about the human person. In the monastery, we learn this lesson not by the variety of our social interactions (you won't find nuns on the front porch of an evening, greeting passersby) but by their intensity. As one sister told me with a smile, "This is God's pressure cooker and he chooses tough pieces of meat!" It's not possible to like everyone all the time, including yourself, but you can love them if you know the truth about them.

Christianity teaches that each human being is a living, moving body organized by a rational, immortal soul formed immediately by God. We are made in the divine image because

God has chosen to share his inner life of knowledge and love with us. All of us share the same origin from God and our last end in God. Because of our spiritual nature, we have needs that are more than material – a hunger for love, meaningful work, and self-transcending worship. Practicing solidarity means a commitment to "the good of all and of each" in this spiritual dimension, too.

By contrast, any social project that gets human dignity seriously wrong (Margaret Sanger's movement and Antifa come to mind) may garner support, but remains fundamentally incapable of creating solidarity. "When man does not recognize in himself and in others the value and grandeur of the human person," warns John Paul II, "he effectively deprives himself of the possibility of benefiting from his humanity and of entering into that relationship of solidarity and communion with others for which God created him."

In other words, if we see our neighbors as less than fully human – if immigrants are useful objects and cheap labor, if refugees and the unborn are an inconvenience or threat, if the elderly or racial minorities are invisible to us – we cannot spend ourselves for their good in any genuine way. Whatever we may gain in the short term (more power, more money, more free time) is ultimately a kind of death for our souls, intended as we are for "solidarity and communion."

Anne Goetze,
The Blue Pail

WITH OUR GODLIKE spiritual nature come the power of free will and the possibility of freely choosing evil, the moral defect called sin. Sin causes alienation from God and from one another, producing what John Paul II calls "a wound in man's inmost self." We have not lost the divine image, or its dignity, but we have misused the Father's gift like the prodigal son who went into a far country.

If you want an example of sisterly solidarity, try examining your conscience sitting in line for Confession alongside women who know your faults better than you do. (Do nuns

Anne Goetze,
Joy

The accumulated sins of individuals can create longstanding injustices in our communities that obstruct the common good and are difficult to repair; this is *social sin*. The real responsibility for the evils of racism, abortion, human trafficking, and destructive consumerism deeply set in our communities lies in the secret places of human hearts. Unless we ponder this truth, we won't understand the value of even a single heart taken from the power of the evil one and given to God.

THE GOOD NEWS of the gospel is that the false solidarity of sin has been overcome by the truth of Christ's solidarity with us: Each one of us, writes John Paul II, "is included in the mystery of redemption, and through this mystery Christ has united himself with each one forever."

really have so many sins, you ask? The late archbishop Fulton J. Sheen supposedly said that "hearing nuns' confessions is like being stoned to death with popcorn." Apparently he thought that what we lack in gravity we make up for in quantity.)

Sin also complicates the picture of human solidarity. We are all really responsible for all; but when all of us fail in our thoughts, words, and actions, our "solidarity" in sin becomes a dark caricature of what should be our firm and persevering commitment to the good. Classic Christian wisdom teaches that every sin has roots in one of the Seven Deadlies: pride, lust, anger, envy, gluttony, sloth, and greed. That's why even "popcorn" sins can be symptoms of big wounds in our souls and communities.

When "the Word became flesh" (John 1:14), the eternal Son personally assumed everything we are and have in body and soul except sin. At the same time, the natural dignity of every human person increased in an astonishing way. We are now joined to God by family ties and, by the bond of grace, intimately associated in Christ's self-gift to the Father on behalf of the world, the mystery of his cross. *His* is the human heart given to God on our behalf.

Who Christ is and what he has done shape the common good profoundly. The very meaning of human flourishing changes when, by the grace of baptism, we gain a created participation in the uncreated life of God. This is how *divine* life is the fullest possible meaning of *human* life: "The grace of Christ," says the

1994 Catechism of the Catholic Church, "is the gratuitous gift that God makes to us of his own life, infused by the Holy Spirit into our soul to heal it of sin and to sanctify it."

Redemption also reveals a new way for us to practice solidarity. Now, in imitation of Christ and moved by his grace, we can lay down our lives for love of others – whether as a mother, a nun, or a martyr. Solidarity thus becomes a participation in the life-giving sacrifice of Christ (John 12:24).

"In the light of faith, solidarity seeks to go beyond itself, to take on the specifically Christian dimensions of total gratuity, forgiveness, and reconciliation," John Paul II explains. "One's neighbor must therefore be loved, even if an enemy, with the same love with which the Lord loves him or her; and for that person's sake one must be ready for sacrifice, even the ultimate one."

Solidarity that goes "beyond itself" like this in forgiveness and reconciliation cannot be grounded in just any definition of love, certainly not in trendy or therapeutic ones. The specifically Christian form carries the radically sacrificial impress of the Sacred Heart of Jesus: when a mother like Saint Gianna Beretta Molla gives her life to carry her unborn child to term; when a priest like Saint Maximilian Kolbe volunteers to take another man's place in a hunger bunker at Auschwitz; and when a child like Saint Maria Goretti forgives her murderer, lovingly calling him to conversion.

All this heroism, from great deeds to the unsung acts of daily Christian life, is accomplished in us by "the same love with which the Lord loves" infused into our hearts by the Holy Spirit. Only divine life can place our natural capacity for self-giving on a supernatural trajectory like this. Christlike solidarity requires much, much more of us than do any of its cheap imitations. What it demands is real holiness made ours by grace.

THE POINT IS THAT EACH of us must walk Christ's path of self-sacrificial love however he leads us. When you grasp this truth, you can begin to understand what the self-gift of solidarity means for a cloistered nun. This life is at the heart of what it means to love and heal the human family because we are all really responsible for all not just in this life, but also before God in the next: *you did it to Me* (Matt. 25).

The life of intercession and adoration in a monastery recalls the world to its highest purpose, seeking God. This priority is the foundation and goal of everything John Paul II taught the world about solidarity: "The apex of [social] development," he writes, "is the exercise of the right and duty to seek God, to know him and to live in accordance with that knowledge."

Perhaps this is what the perplexed need to hear: Hidden solidarity is real because the life of grace is real. We are all united as members of Christ's mystical body, each in creative fidelity to our own vocations. God brings his image to perfection in us slowly, offering a thousand small ways to follow Christ in solidarity with our neighbors. Let us, then, give our all too human hearts to God and to one another. ➤

> **Christlike solidarity requires much more of us than do any of its cheap imitations.**

AN INTERVIEW WITH BRAULIO CONDORI

Acts 2 in Bolivia

What does a community inspired by the first church in Jerusalem look like in an indigenous Andean context? Braulio Condori, the founder of such a community in Bolivia, talked to *Plough*'s Fida Meier about his group's mission and story.

Street market in El Alto, near where the community has its farm

Plough: Your community, Amigos del Bruderhof, is inspired by (though independent from) the Bruderhof, the community that publishes *Plough*. With a difference: You're situated in the indigenous culture of Bolivia's Altiplano. For twenty years, you've been living in full community of goods in the spirit of Acts 2 and 4. How does your Aymara heritage shape the community's life and mission?

Braulio Condori: We are all people of the Aymara culture. Our mother tongue is Aymara, although we also speak Spanish.

Many values in our indigenous culture are also important in the Christian life. Nonviolence, for example, is important in both our culture and our faith, and we hold to it.

We also try to keep our Aymara customs. Here are some examples: *Ayni*, or mutual aid, is summed up by the saying "Today for you, tomorrow for me." *Minca* means I help you, and you give me some of what you earned or harvested during the day. *Trueque*, or barter, is also important: we exchange potatoes for cheese, or onions for sugar.

Braulio Condori is the founder of Amigos del Bruderhof, a small intentional Christian community in La Paz and El Alto, Bolivia.

We want to be part of our locality, so we invite neighbors to our plantings and harvests, returning the favor later (*ayni*) or paying them with produce we have on hand (*minca*). We interact a lot with the people of the village near our Altiplano farm. If there is a meeting, we bring juice or a light meal and share the gospel of Jesus Christ through our testimonies and singing. In La Paz, we mostly meet our neighbors at our market stand. People tell us confidentially about problems they face, and we encourage them with words of hope and forgiveness.

It is also important that our community models simplicity and is not perceived as wealthier or living at a higher standard than our neighbors. On the Altiplano, we only installed electricity in 2013, long after everyone around us had it.

How do you make your living?

In the city market, we sell supplies for schools, offices, and universities, as well as children's toys. We also have a farm on the Altiplano, about twenty kilometers outside the city, where we grow food for our community. We raise milk cows, hens, guinea pigs, and sheep and cultivate potatoes, yucca, broad beans, and other legumes.

What does your community's outreach look like?

We host retreats, camps, and conferences, especially supporting community-centered organizations and gatherings of indigenous people from throughout South and Central America. Recently, we provided food and lodging for a conference of the *Centro de Capacitación Misionera* (Center for Missionary Training). People came from Panama, Mexico, Peru, Colombia, Brazil, Argentina, Chile, and Uruguay, as well as other regions of Bolivia. Some of them were very interested in

our community and in the early Christians, and wanted further contact. On one occasion, Samuel, one of our members, showed indigenous people from many countries how we cultivate our land with a team of oxen. He demonstrated that communal work is possible even in today's world.

We also get other churches involved: Lutherans, Nazarenes, Pentecostals, Adventists, and Quakers. They participate materially and spiritually in our conferences. Our goal is to sow the spirit of the first Christians in their hearts and inspire them to strengthen community within their own churches. But most of our communication with others is on a personal level. These friends spread the message to others, who spread it to yet more people.

Several young people from the Bruderhof lived and worked with us for a few months or years between 1995 and 2014. There were also years when we requested that no Bruderhof youth stay with us. We wanted to show that living in community is our own choice, based on Acts 2 and 4, not an imposed foreign model or another North American evangelization effort.

How did your community start?

My father was a pastor in the Evangelical Quaker church in La Paz, Bolivia. As a young man, I supported him, participating enthusiastically as a youth leader. But I wasn't satisfied, and often wondered how I could live out my Christian discipleship in practical ways, loving my neighbor as myself. I read about the early Christians in the Book of Acts many times. Each time, the question arose in my heart: Was it possible to live like that today?

A fellow Quaker pastor first told me about the Bruderhof. When I learned that there were people living the same faith as the early Christians, it inspired me to start living in community in my own city. A local Mennonite

Braulio, his wife, Maria, and their son, Pablo

gave me the address of the Darvell Bruderhof in England, and after a few years of correspondence, I invited several Bruderhof members to visit us in Bolivia in 1995. I had always thought that missionaries needed a special place to stay, but in their case there was none of this. They had no problem sharing our food and customs. The simple life of these brothers and sisters rekindled my wish to start a Christian community. They invited us to visit the Bruderhof, so a few months later seven of us adults and a baby visited Darvell.

After a month, we returned to Bolivia, where problems erupted in our church. I was called to a meeting of the national church council where they accused me of following a strange gospel. Then they expelled me from the church. That was my darkest and saddest night. I felt I had lost everything. Later, a letter arrived forbidding me from entering their churches, and this was circulated to each congregation. I tried to visit, but was rejected. Only the small church where I had grown up was willing to take me in.

At this difficult time, we founded our community in a rented house in El Alto, a city on the outskirts of La Paz. Later, we acquired a property in the tropical district of Los Yungas, about five hours' drive from La Paz, where we shared our faith in Christian community for three years.

In 1999, most of the brothers and sisters decided to return to their former lives. This again was a painful time. At one point, in July 1999, I was the only one willing to make a commitment to full membership, supported by several brothers and sisters who did not want to be full members but would continue doing things with us. Finally another brother, Samuel, who had been a high school senior at the time of the breakup, became a committed member. The joy this brought helped me leave the past behind and look forward. Over the next years, Samuel and I each married and started our families. Our community began to grow again. At present, these two families are committed members, and there are six families of associate members who support our vision of living out the gospel of Jesus Christ in a practical life.

What is your relationship today to your former church, which had expelled you?

One of our most important experiences was when we forgave the leaders who expelled us from their church. Forgiveness is the essence of Christianity. Without it, a person rots inside. So we decided we needed to take the first step, and started visiting ailing family members of these people. At their bedsides, our past disagreements fell away and we reconciled. Today, most of the pastors of that church are our friends. They visit to encourage us on our way of community, and we converse like brothers and sisters. We give them books, and they donate money to help out.

We have also made every effort to heal broken relationships with former members who left our community. Forgiveness starts right away, but sometimes takes time to come to fruition. They have slowly drawn closer, and now we are good friends. Our forgiveness and love must be expressed continually. We can't say "it's all good" with words unless we follow up with deeds. So we call them and sometimes they tell us about their problems. If we can help, we do, even if we can't give much. We invite them to our conferences, where they participate with enthusiasm.

At the end of 2019, there were protests sparked by the presidential election results and the subsequent ouster of Evo Morales, who had been Bolivia's first indigenous president. How did this turmoil affect your community?

This is not the first time we have lived through unrest. El Alto is a city full of internal refugees, and uprisings are common. Over the years, the abuses of various administrations have sparked resistance movements, which we were involved with, even participating in some protests.

Morales did much for the poor and indigenous, but we didn't always agree with him. In 2017, he changed Article 88 of the penal code, which addresses human trafficking, establishing a seven- to twelve-year prison sentence for recruiting people for armed conflicts or religious organizations. We feared that preaching the gospel would be prohibited. If I would invite seekers to my house to share the gospel with them, would this be illegal? As a community, we listen to the voice of God and obey him before these laws, even if that means risking our lives. If we love Jesus, he will guide us in the best way and protect us. And he has continued to do this. After six weeks of popular protest, the new law was overturned.

But you asked about the recent upheaval, when Morales was forced to leave the country. Factions erected roadblocks. People were so desperate for food that there was looting in the markets. Sellers fled with their goods so they wouldn't lose the little capital they had. Because we are part of a union in the market, we support the other vendors. There we were

The community's farm on the Altiplano

together, and we had the opportunity to call for God's protection with prayers and Bible readings. Right there in the market, everyone went down on their knees to ask for protection and peace for our country.

On our farm, Samuel and his wife, Margara, had a similar experience. Our neighbors considered our community a trustworthy place and brought their belongings for safekeeping. Through this, they drew close to us and we could proclaim the gospel by showing them love. Every time we met as a community, we knelt to pray for peace for Bolivia. Getting involved doesn't mean being contaminated by politics. It means spreading the love of Christ in the midst of desperation. It means offering the hope that Jesus is present in every situation.

What is your vision for the future of your community?

Our plans, hopes, and vision are in God's hands. We don't want to write things down on paper. We just want to be attentive to the voice of God and be guided by the spontaneous Spirit. Our vision is to be a community that cannot be hidden, like the city on a hill in Matthew 5:14. ➤

Interview by Fida Meier on January 15, 2020. Translated from Spanish by Coretta Thomson.

ANOTHER LIFE IS POSSIBLE

FOUR STORIES FROM

100 YEARS OF LIFE TOGETHER

CLARE STOBER

With Photography by Danny Burrows

TWO YEARS AGO I BEGAN work on a book to mark the Bruderhof's hundredth anniversary this year. I'd long been interested in the idea of vocation– why and how does a person become convinced of a lifelong calling, with the self-sacrifice and self-surrender that this requires? For the Bruderhof centenary, then, my editors and I decided not to focus on the community's century of history, but rather to tell the vocation stories of the men and women who had joined it. We ambitiously agreed on one hundred stories for one hundred years. I immediately began interviewing my fellow Bruderhof members, asking them to tell why they had chosen this way of life in full Christian community and getting them to share insights gleaned along the way. At the same time I accompanied the British photojournalist Danny Burrows, traveling to ten communities on three continents to capture what our life together looks like. The following four stories are excerpted from the resulting book of one hundred stories and Danny's stunning photographs, titled *Another Life Is Possible: Insights from 100 Years of Life Together*.

Explore the stories or order the book at *AnotherLifeIsPossible.com*.

Clare Stober, *Plough*'s creative director, grew up in a military family and, after college at the Rochester Institute of Technology, cofounded a design and marketing firm in Northern Virginia. Dissatisfied with business success, she joined the Bruderhof in 1992. Her new book, *Another Life Is Possible*, appears in September.

Through prayer and pilgrimage, a South Korean engineer finds her true calling.

1. HYERAN JANG

HYERAN LEARNED TO PRAY from her mother, a devout woman who, after converting to Christianity early in Hyeran's childhood, attended prayer meetings at 4:00 every morning. Prayer formed the background for her childhood, despite her father's atheism and her family's troubles. As a ten-year-old, Hyeran discovered that her father had a mistress and "another family." How could such a situation be resolved? She had no answer beyond her mother's example of constant prayer.

As a teenager, Hyeran's questions about identity also played out against that background of prayer.

I was like Jacob in the Old Testament who always struggled with his identity, and asked: Who am I? And then wrestled with the angel, saying, "I won't let you go until you give me a name." And

then he got the name Israel, his identity, finally.

When I was a teenager, I was not just asking "Who am I?" but I was trying to discover what my identity was in God's Word. How much is God involved in what happens in the world? And then: What should I do for God?

When Hyeran was sixteen, she had a vivid experience of Jesus:

While I was praying, it seemed that a strong wind blew around me, and I was suddenly struck by the feeling that I was a sinner. Then I wept and wept; my sin killed Jesus. That was an experience of being baptized by the Holy Spirit.

At the same time, Hyeran's awareness of the injustices of South Korea's competitive economic and educational system was growing. During a crucial

"I felt like I was on a cliff, and I had to either keep standing there, or jump. I decided to jump – to give up everything."

examination period in high school, a teacher mocked the vocational students headed for Korea's factories: "It bothered me. A teacher should give his students hope and enthusiasm, but he was looking down on them." In protest, and despite being a usually well-behaved student on the school's top academic track, Hyeran refused to take his test.

Her rebellion earned her punishment, both hands beaten with a wooden rod until they were swollen, and meetings with her alarmed parents and school administrators. She eventually gave in. (Later, Hyeran and her teacher found understanding and reconciliation.) "I graduated and went on to university, where I studied urban design and engineering. I had great hopes that we could change cities, especially housing and transportation systems. They weren't built with people's best

interests in mind, and so many people suffer in them."

Hyeran had to fight to hold her own in a field heavily dominated by men. As well as being a woman, she was also the only Christian in her college cohort. Social life was defined by heavy drinking, dirty jokes, and selfish individualism. Seniors demanded that underclassmen address them as God. One initiation rite involved "duck walking," a hike up a mountainside in squatting position, with their hands touching their ears.

After graduating, Hyeran joined a group that was praying for the reunification of North and South Korea. She helped plan a peace village to be built in the demilitarized zone between them and publish a magazine about reunification, justice, and community.

All photographs courtesy of Danny Burrows (unless otherwise noted)

Suddenly one thought came to my heart strongly. I felt that God wanted me to pray for our nation for a whole year. So I decided to quit my job to spend one year in pilgrimage and prayer, traveling around Korea and visiting convents, abbeys, orphanages, and communities. I wanted to know how God was working in Korea, and I also wanted to find the place where God was calling me to be. During that year I was inspired by reading the Gospels, and was deeply moved by God's love for this world.

After that year, Hyeran visited Beech Grove Bruderhof, which she had learned about through her publishing work. She stayed there a while, then visited a few other communities in Europe, and then Danthonia, Australia. It was there that she decided to become a member.

I felt like I was on a cliff, and I had to either keep standing there, or jump. I decided to jump–to give up everything. After I made my vows, I was told: "Hyeran, now you belong to us, and we to you. You will be taken care of for the rest of your life." I wept. I had longed to find a place where such a mutual commitment is possible for so many years, but never found it.

I had such joy losing myself. I don't want my life to be about what I'm doing, or what I planned and then achieved. What I really want is that God's kingdom affects everybody's life, not only my life.

In early 2019, Hyeran moved back to South Korea with a few others to found a small Bruderhof community there.

∧
A riotous tag game through the Australian paddocks around Danthonia, the community at which Hyeran arrived.

A Philadelphia businessman, troubled by the contradictions of capitalism, traveled to Paraguay to see if a life based on love was possible.

2. TOM POTTS
1908–1999

TOM POTTS WAS BORN into a prominent Philadelphia Quaker family. He went to Haverford College, where he was a fullback on the soccer team, and then started working at the steel warehousing company his extended family owned. During World War II, the steel industry was regulated in service of the war effort and Tom, who took Quakerism's traditional pacifism seriously, refused to cooperate. Instead, he went to work for the American Friends Service Committee, and was assigned to manage Civilian Public Service camps during the war as an alternative to military service. Florrie, whom he had met and married in 1934, came with him.

After the war, Tom and Florrie resumed their life in Philadelphia: Sunday gatherings at the Friends Meeting and private schools for their three children. As Florrie later described, "we were

on a lot of committees and working with good causes, race relations and sharecroppers. But nothing specially came of it." Through their Quaker connections, they met and eventually hosted members of the Bruderhof who were traveling in the United States fundraising for the hospital in Paraguay. Tom and Florrie's decision to travel there and then to become members of the Bruderhof is best explained by Tom in an open letter that he sent to the Friends Meeting in 1952:

For all my adult life I have been frustrated by the contradiction between ordinary American life and the impossible teaching of Jesus' second commandment, "Love thy neighbor as thyself." I make out all right during the week: I have a good job and I am part owner of a steel warehouse. We have a most congenial working group and

<<
A Community
Playthings workshop,
the Bruderhof business
that Tom Potts led for
over four decades.

> ## "Unbelieving, I took my wife and three children ten thousand miles to see if this life could be true. And it was."

enjoy the game of competing in the marketplace for the available business. We advertise honestly, we charge fair prices, we are concerned about good employee relations, we have a Christmas party, we give generously to the community chest, and we have a profit-sharing scheme. But do I love my neighbor as myself? Am I concerned for the clerk who has come to work in the streetcar while I drive a big car? Do I give the community chest just what I don't need anyway? Do I share the profit in reality, or do I save a big percentage for my old age, before the distribution? Yet, if I gave it all away, what would my family and I live on? How foolish can you get?

But Jesus did not say, "Love your neighbor after taking care of yourself." Then on Sunday when I go to meeting for worship of the Society of Friends I realize again and again that all men are children of God and brothers to each other. But what do I do about it? Periodically Friends ask themselves searching queries such as: "Do you keep to simplicity and moderation in your manner of living, in your pursuit of business?" We have two cars. We send our children to private schools and buy them all the clothes and incidentals they want for keeping up with the Joneses. We get for ourselves pretty much what we want. Is that simplicity? How about the business? To what purpose would I spend my major time and energy for the next (and last) twenty years in building our business to two, three, ten times its present size? I would double my income, triple my worries, and perhaps donate more to good causes. But would the donations of money, however large, serve to bring the kingdom here on earth, as would the widow's mite of my waning energies devoted to a Christian system?

America is rapidly being taken over by the military. I pay a healthy income tax, far more than I am able to give to the Friends Peace Committee. Yet another query says: "Do you faithfully maintain our testimony against preparation for war as inconsistent with the spirit and teachings of Christ?"

Our social and economic system is based on the premise that if each looks out for himself the end result will benefit everyone. But does it? What about the third of our nation who are still ill-fed, ill-housed, and ill-clothed, not to speak of the millions upon millions in the underdeveloped parts of the world? The query says, "What are you doing to create a social and economic system which will so function as to sustain and enrich life for all?"

The contradiction is everywhere apparent. In order not to feel completely frustrated during these times of soul-searching, I have long reasoned that Jesus must have been setting up an ideal towards which mankind should work and might attain in a few thousand years. And then we discovered the Society of Brothers [as the Bruderhof was known at the time]. They said they were trying to live by the Sermon on the Mount. Traveling brothers told us of the communities in Paraguay, Uruguay, and England, where more than 850 people are living a life of complete sharing. Each person surrenders his will, his talents, his possessions to God, and together they seek a life of true unity based on love for all.

Unbelieving, I took my wife and three children 10,000 miles to see if it could be true. And it was. Their social and economic system is based on the premise that if each one, having faith in God, looks out for his brother, the end result will benefit all, including himself. Men and women from eighteen countries, formerly from all walks of life and all rungs of the social ladder, are living together as brothers and sisters, helping one another, working hard, and experiencing deep spiritual joy. How can I do anything else but settle my affairs and join the work of spreading the news that it is possible to live in accord with the spiritual laws of the universe here and now?

My contribution will be small. But however small, I shall be

advancing a practical way of living which does, in actuality and in the words of the query, accept all without discrimination because of race, creed, or social class, and where all are treated as brothers and equals.

And so Tom and Florrie's life in community began. When Woodcrest, the first American location, was founded in 1954, the Potts family moved there and Tom was asked to manage the community's woodworking business. Florrie was his secretary, working at a desk facing his and helping to organize the sales staff. At that time Community Playthings' product line consisted of wooden building blocks and a limited selection of classroom furnishings which were marketed to schools and nurseries. The manufacturing facility was primitive and the community was in debt. Under Tom's

leadership over the next four decades, Community Playthings became a well-regarded, internationally distributed company selling wooden toys, play equipment, and classroom furniture. In the late 1970s, when children with disabilities began to be integrated into classrooms, teachers from a school near one of the Community Playthings workshops requested chairs modified for these new students. Under Tom's leadership this opening developed into a new business, Rifton Equipment, which now matches Community Playthings in size.

Together, the businesses provided not only income to support the communities in the United States and England, but meaningful work for its members. The core purpose of the community was always more important to Tom than profit: if sales were high and the overtime required to make the

∧
Caring customer service, Tom believed, was at the heart of Community Playthings' success.

>
Rifton Equipment,
which manufactures
aids for people with
disabilities, grew
out of Community
Playthings in 1977.

>>
Community
Playthings' stackable,
molded maple
plywood chairs in
the curing oven for
the environmentally
friendly finish.

products started interfering with community life, Tom would quietly put some orders in a desk drawer to wait for calmer times. He always took care that the operation of the businesses reflected the community's values: that customers and vendors were treated with respect and that the design and manufacture of the products reflected love for the children who would use them. (Tom's three business principles were quality, quality, and quality.) He felt accountable to the community membership for his business decisions, once apologizing in tears during a church meeting for spending money on a new marketing approach that had failed to pay off.

Tom was a humble man who never took himself too seriously. Hearing himself described as an expert he once said, "Oh, you know what an expert is. An ex is a has-been, and a spurt is just a drip under pressure." Known to the children of the community as "Wolfie," he would interrupt a business call or meeting to growl theatrically if a child looked in the door of his office (as they were welcome to do, knowing that there was candy hidden in the desk).

And then, after four decades of managing a successful business, Tom handed over responsibility for it to a younger coworker, John Rhodes, who had been learning from him for some years. Too old to lead a business, but still full of life, Tom went to work in the Rifton Equipment shop, threading straps on the sandals of mobility equipment. A visitor to the shop once asked him about his work. "You could say I am assembling this part," Tom said, "but what I am really doing is

thinking about the child who will use it one day."

Tom and Florrie never lost some aspects of their Quaker upbringing. Evening gatherings at their home ended at 10:00, "Quaker midnight." Quakers are "plain people" and the Pottses loved simplicity: anyone was welcome at their table at noon on Sunday (and many came) when they served "Sunday soup" made from leftover vegetables from the community kitchen. And they addressed each other in the Quaker manner as "thee" and "thou" with the great love that defined their relationship. "Now here comes Florrie," Tom would say as his wife of sixty-four years approached. "Doesn't she look lovely?"

A college student strives to carry on his father's legacy of working for justice.

3. RUBÉN AYALA

GROWING UP IN the predominantly white Bruderhof, Rubén was only vaguely aware that he was different. Then, in the second grade, his class made a field trip to a nearby public school, and a kid on the playground there called him the n-word. Today, a senior at City College in Harlem—one of the nation's most diverse campuses in its best-known African-American neighborhood—he says he is still learning who he is. Far more importantly, his eyes are being opened to the realities of inequality and injustice, and he is learning through real-life experiences how the people most affected think these injustices can be overcome.

Rubén's first teacher was his father, a tough-as-nails Puerto Rican who was raised on the streets of Brooklyn and went to prison at seventeen. After being released ten years later,

he struggled with drugs and alcohol, and ended up at The Bowery Mission, a Christian organization that helps people escape homelessness and addiction. There he met a group of volunteers from the Bruderhof. After several years of off-and-on visiting, he joined. In 1993, he married Emilie, who had been raised within the community.

When Rubén was three, recurring battles with alcoholism led his father to leave the family and the community, and for the next several years, his mother raised him on her own. When he was ten, his father returned, and the family was reunited.

Only now, as an adult, does Rubén realize how much his father shaped his cultural identity in those critical years. A lot of it he simply absorbed:

<<
Evening worship
with members of the
Harlem community on
their rooftop deck

> Rubén's favorite mementos from his father: a Mets hat, a Roberto Clemente jersey, and a photo with his father's hands on his shoulders.

He loved to cook, and in summer he'd invite anyone who wanted to join us in front of our house. He'd turn up his music – salsa, merengue, reggae, hip-hop – and then start preparing the food: arroz con gandules, arroz con pollo, octopus salad, and all kinds of things. Mom, who also likes to cook, would make dessert. Afterward we'd play stickball for hours, while my dad's cat, Brooklyn, and my dog, Shea, would chase each other and fight and add to the general craziness.

But just as much was transmitted through intentional lessons:

Anyway, one day when I was in sixth grade he pulls down this book and says, "You need to read this." It was Chancellor Williams's *The Destruction of Black Civilization*, an Afrocentric history of the colonization of Africa. It's openly biased, but important because it's from a perspective you won't find in any standard histories.

I told him, "I'm not reading that big fat thing." But he was like, "Yeah, you are." I did plow my way through it over time, and, more than any other book, it's the one that got me interested in my major, history. It got me interested in digging for the truth.

Rubén's father also opened his eyes to many social justice issues:

Take the Puerto Rican nationalists of the sixties and seventies. That was a cause Dad believed in, and he didn't just show it by the flag that was always hanging in our living room. He was passionate about the history of oppression on the island. He told me about the mass sterilization of Puerto Rican women in the 1950s, and about the repression of the Young Lords, who started out as a street gang in Chicago but became known for their activism.

Another thing that concerned Dad was mass incarceration and capital punishment. As someone who had been incarcerated, he was set on raising awareness of what he called the "rotten-ass system."

The war and famine in Darfur was another major concern of his, and in 2008 our family traveled to the Sudan to see what was going on firsthand. We went with an organization our community had donated to, though Dad was just as interested in the history of the region, which is regarded as the birthplace of the Nubian kingdom. That trip opened my eyes to the

> ## "Show solidarity in the sense of being willing to learn, rather than always wanting to be the teacher."

reality of suffering in many ways, but there's one particular incident I'll never forget: in one village we stopped at, a woman tried to give my mother her baby. She literally begged Mom to take the baby back to America with us, and said, "He's just going to die if he grows up here." I can still see her face.

By 2010, Rubén's father was struggling with his addictions again and decided to leave once more.

I was in the eighth grade, and struggling with who I was in this community where almost everybody else had two parents, and things seemed to be going fine. I was always popular at school and had good grades, but I was all beat up inside and would often get angry at home.

But even if his father wasn't physically present, Rubén says the memory of his lessons continued to guide him:

I began to realize why my dad had exposed me to so many things and told me so many stories about his life. He had wanted to make me aware of things I would one day face on my own. In fact, he once said as much: "These are my experiences, and they made me who I am, but you're different than me, so you're going to have to fight your own battles and figure things out for yourself."

During his father's absence, Rubén says it was his mother who exerted the single most powerful influence on his developing view of the world:

Mom's family is German-American, from the Midwest. Culturally, she had nothing in common with my father, but in terms of her concerns, she was the same. For example: she'd often drive me to neighbors and friends outside the community. We would have dinner with them and discuss things. One woman I especially remember worked with juvenile delinquents. Mom made sure I listened to this woman about her experiences with the courts.

In late 2012, Rubén's father returned. He died at the Bruderhof several months later, of heart disease. Two years later Rubén graduated from high school. He spent a gap year in Australia before moving to New York City to go to college. He became a full member of the Bruderhof in April 2019.

Not surprisingly, living in Harlem has brought to life the stories his father used to tell him in a way he never could have imagined from the protected vantage point of his childhood:

I used to think, "Wow, Dad went through all this stuff? That's crazy." But now it doesn't surprise me

at all. The things that happened to him are not so far out. They happen all the time. Racism is still alive and well. It's wrong. It's maddening. It seems archaic. But the particulars aren't illegal, so it goes on and on, and millions of people are trapped in it.

Asked for his insights on how injustice can be fought, Rubén says that one of the biggest obstacles to progress is people's inability – or unwillingness – to admit that certain problems exist.

Take something like racism, or more specifically, police brutality and the way it affects people of color. To many whites, it's just a made-up thing. They so badly wish it was over and done with that they only see what they want to see.

But hey, I live in Harlem, and I've witnessed it. I've seen a boy riding a bike, and five cops jumping on him and just slamming him to the ground. Or take a movement like Black Lives Matter. I've heard people dismiss it by saying, "All lives matter." Of course every life matters, but that's a cynical response. Or they say they get the basic issue, but not the anger behind it. They seem unable to see that there might be a cause for that anger, and that you can't just condemn it and hope it will go away.

Unless you have had a personal experience connected with a life-and-death issue like this, maybe you shouldn't make too many sweeping statements. And if you don't have that connection, maybe you should take time to listen to someone who is actually affected by it.

I think justice can begin when people are no longer trapped by external circumstances or victimized by the power other people hold over them. For those of us who already have those freedoms, I think it's a call to action: to respect the culture and history of whoever is disenfranchised. And to show solidarity in the sense of being willing to learn, rather than always wanting to be the teacher. And to make sacrifices so that others can have a chance at getting ahead.

People – I'm talking about all races here – tend to congregate with their own kind, with others who have similar backgrounds and life experiences. And so the cycle continues. It's just a fact that if you can't understand the people "on the other side," the easiest solution is to ignore them. But the problem is that in the long run, you end up being scared of each other.

My dad's feeling for justice came from a personal place. His anger and his energy came from what he experienced as a child and young man. And yet he ended up joining the Bruderhof. That used to puzzle me. Now I see that he deliberately chose to live in a way where he could break down the walls that separate people. I think joining the community was a deliberate move toward that. In fact, he told me multiple times, "Yeah, I believe that people should live together and work out their differences." So even though he knew what racism was, he still wasn't scared to live with white people or to marry a white woman. I honestly think that at least in part, it was to break down the barriers of inequality, first of all for himself, because he didn't want to be trapped in a world of us versus them. He was looking for true justice, the kind built on love and community.

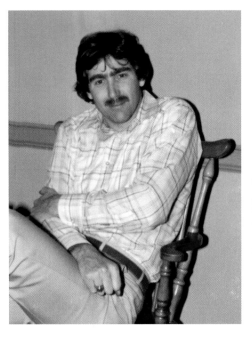

A New York professional searches for a comprehensive answer.

4. BILL CLEVA

BY 1978, FIVE YEARS after Bill had graduated from Notre Dame, he was working as a civil engineer on the ninety-second floor of the World Trade Center and possessed every material trapping that was to have guaranteed happiness. But two years later he quit his job for good, "totally finished" with the corporate world and his yuppie lifestyle. The near-catastrophe at Three Mile Island, plus a scandal involving the Filipino dicta-tor Ferdinand Marcos, Westinghouse, and construction of that country's first nuclear plant, played a decisive role:

I was not just disillusioned. It was a much deeper restlessness–a divine dissatisfaction that can only be explained as an intervention from God. I didn't will it on myself, and it didn't feel very divine at the time. My family, colleagues, and friends thought I was crazy. Some stopped talking to me altogether.

In 1994, after years of intense searching for something that would fill the void in his heart, Bill became a member of the Bruderhof. Reflecting on what he found, he says:

My initial infatuation with the outer workings of the community was before very long swallowed up by the overriding demands of trying to put Jesus' teachings into daily practice. The sacrifices never lessen. Yet here is a movement of brotherly and sisterly community that has been sustained for one hundred years by nothing but the fidelity of otherwise flawed people, and by the corresponding leading of the Spirit. I am not aware of any other such comprehensive answer to the ongoing need of the human condition. ➤

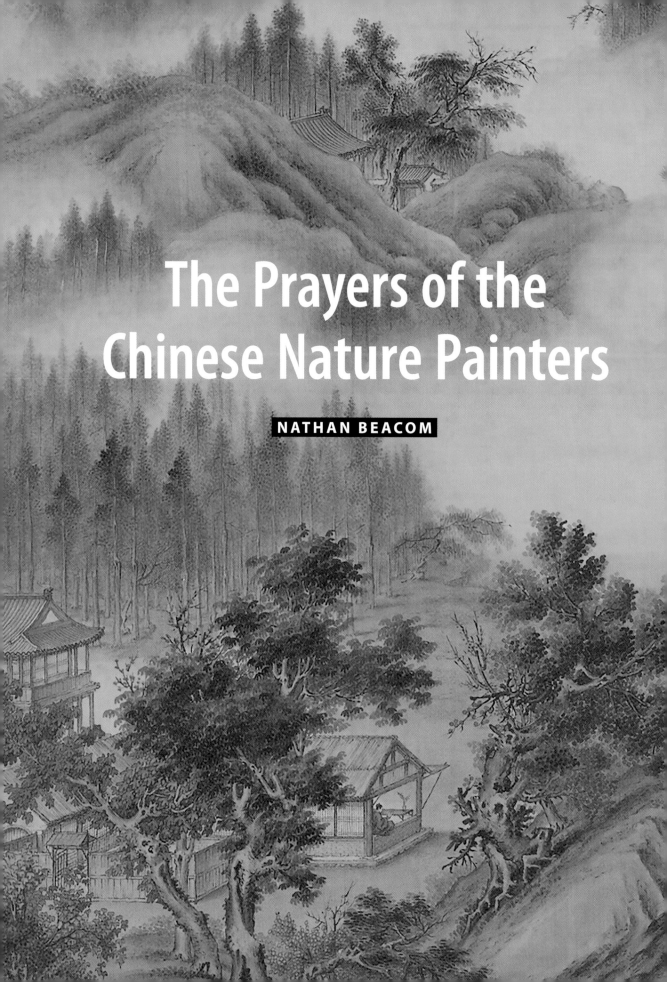

The Prayers of the Chinese Nature Painters

NATHAN BEACOM

A DISTORTED GOLD CAT wags its paw on the other side of a bubbling aquarium. The smells of cashew chicken and egg drop soup mingle with the Chinese-instrument covers of pop songs coming from the ceiling. You know the scene. In the back of the room, behind the paper lanterns, hangs a landscape painting in shades of emerald and topaz. Some mountains, a river, maybe a few cranes flying. Nice.

But the great works of Chinese nature painting are not just nice; they are not even just paintings. They are often poetry, philosophy, and prayer all at once. In this tradition, painting is the fruit of contemplation, and, when this is true, it is also a kind of prayer. In creating, the artist identifies the spiritual meaning of things and seeks to help the viewer to see them too. This art can help the viewer to pray with nature in a new way, to love it, to see in it something of the divine.

IN THE LATE NORTHERN AND SOUTHERN Dynasties, or around the turn of the sixth century, in Western terms, the writer Xie He composed his famous "Six Principles" of painting. The first of them calls for *qiyun shengdong*, "spirit-resonance showing life-motion," usually understood to mean that a painter needs to capture the essential character of his or her subject in order to make it come alive in the artwork. Without spirit-resonance, a painting feels static, flat, and opaque. The goal of Chinese landscape painting is not mere accuracy of illustration, but capturing the spirit of a place, which requires a process of contemplation where the painter comes to understand the poetic meaning of the subject.

Jacques Maritain, the Catholic philosopher, thought this Chinese notion of spiritual

Previous spread: Lang Shining, *Landscape*, detail, eighteenth century

resonance pointed to something fundamental about art in general. Poetry, in his view, is the spring of all art, which is about seeing analogies. If we think of a big old oak as proud and noble, we are seeing an analogy between the tree and the human spirit. An artist can pick out those connections well, and make something (a song, a poem, a painting) that communicates them. An artist can show that mountains have something in common with honor, that a wren shares something with a joyful heart, that a breeze at night is not unlike a heartbreak.

Guo Xi, a painter and writer who lived some four centuries after Xie He, indicated that the painter's ability to see the spiritual meaning of things depended on his or her own spiritual character: "A virtuous man takes delight in landscapes so that in a rustic retreat he may nourish his nature, amid the carefree play of streams and rocks, he may take delight." To see in nature the qualities of excellence and virtue, the artist must be attuned to receive them.

In the time of Guo Xi, perhaps no one better embodied painting as a spiritual practice than the mountain man Fan Kuan. With his rough clothes, grey-flecked beard, tanned and weather-beaten skin, and open face etched by deep thought, he was known as generous and easygoing, a lover of mountains, wine, and, above all, the Way – the path in life and harmony with nature known as the Tao.

As a young man, he left the wealth and hypocrisy of the city for a contemplative life in the Qinling mountains. As excellent as he was at copying the old masters, he came to feel that time spent with nature itself was the only way to paint it authentically. He also seems to have wanted to escape the pretensions of the artistic circles in the city in order to live a more

---

Nathan Beacom is a writer from Des Moines, Iowa. His work on agriculture, the environment, and other subjects has appeared in Civil Eats, America Magazine, *and* Front Porch Republic.

All images public domain

Fan Kuan,
*Travelers by
Mountains and
Streams*, circa
AD 1000

Lang Shining, leaf from *Immortal Blossoms of an Eternal Spring*, seventeenth century

walls above us. As art historian Richard Barnhart has written, some commentators of Fan Kuan's own age thought that the closeness and strength of the scene, which crowds and presses upon the viewer, is meant to be an embodiment of *wu*, or martial virtue. Contemporary scholars like Wen Fong have seen in the tripartite composition a Confucian message that all things are harmoniously ordered: the foreground might be seen as the small realm of man, the middle ground the space of nature, and the mountains shoot up to represent the divine.

These mountains are not painted as they would look in a photograph; each choice of brushstroke, of shade, of placement is made for a reason – to depict the scene as filled with meaning and memory. The Tao is not reducible to human language, the classic Taoist texts hold. Art, however, speaks in another way. Analysis of the painting is not as good as merely spending time with it.

This is part of the reason why classical Chinese painters so often abandon normal limitations of perspective and unity of composition; they are emphasizing a scene not as it presents itself to the eye, but as it inhabits the soul. In a photograph, our vision is limited by the lens. In a painting like Fan Kuan's, we see the mountain, not as it appears from one vantage point at one time, but as it appears to a man who has walked among its nooks and crannies, loved it, and come to associate it with the various events of his life. Guo Xi called this

authentic life. In his hermitage, he watched the course of the seasons, was buffeted by the extremes of mountain snows and rainstorms, and came to know the cliffs and valleys in each of their moods. He lived in and with this landscape, fished its streams, hunted in its valleys, and meditated on its prominences.

His life of meditation in the mountains was an effort to become one with things, and his *Travelers by Mountains and Streams* (previous page) displays the result of years of discerning the spiritual qualities in the highlands of Shaanxi.

Towering peaks rise in the mist behind the middle ground, where tiny travelers magnify the majesty of the heights. A third layer of close, craggy stones separates us, the viewers, from the pathway of the travelers and makes us feel as if we were at the edges of the scene; we seem to peer over the stones at the vastness of mountain freedom of perspective the "angle of totality." For the artist who lived in these mountains, each part of the scene has become a friend and reveals a personality.

Fan Kuan sees in the Qinling peaks fortitude, long-suffering patience, cheerfulness, purity, hospitality, and austere beauty. He reveals fortitude in the unshakable mountains; patience in the bent, sturdy trees; cheerfulness in the travelers; purity in the thin waterfall that splits the cliff face; and hospitality in the tiny temple hidden in the forest. This is what Maritain called the "interpenetration of man and nature."

When we look at this painting, we enter a kind of conversation with its painter, an encounter between our beliefs and associations. Fan Kuan invites us to contemplate the spiritual significance of the beautiful country he knew. His heart resonates with the landscape and, through his work, our hearts as well.

Maritain held that this spiritual resonance in art does not extend laterally alone, between one thing on earth and another, but vertically, to the divine. In a similar spirit, perhaps, the apostle Paul writes that the invisible attributes of God, even his eternal power, have been clearly seen in things that are made (Rom. 1:20); Chinese landscape painting has a wonderful way of revealing this.

CENTURIES AFTER FAN KUAN passed beyond the Qinling mountains, another painter came to China from across the sea. Trained in the studios of Italy, Giuseppe Castiglione (1688–1766) would become the court painter of three Chinese rulers and the dear friend of the Qianlong Emperor, who praised his virtue and goodness as much as his artistry. He is remembered in China as master painter Lang Shining.

Lang Shining was trained by the Baroque painter Andrea Pozzo, still famous for the masterful illusionist ceiling of the Church of Saint Ignatius in Rome. Other European artists had tried and failed to bring the vision of the West to China, but only Lang Shining had both the talent and understanding to harmonize the spirit of the Celestial Kingdom with that of Christian Europe.

Lang Shining, leaf from *Flowers and Birds*, seventeenth century

Lang Shining was a Jesuit brother, and the teaching of Saint Ignatius to "go and seek God in all things" can be observed in his artistic as well as his pastoral work. Arriving in China in the time of the Kangxi Emperor, he encountered a ruler who felt a real affinity between his own Confucianism and the teaching of the Jesuits, and wanted to encourage a dialogue between the two traditions. Likewise, the Jesuits found much to admire in Confucianism. The notion of finding God in all things is a key touchpoint with the spiritual vision of the Chinese landscape artists, so intent upon meditating on divinity in nature. The poet Zhang Ruitu (1570–1641), from Fujian, wrote these lines about the similarities between Chinese thought and the teachings of the Jesuit Guilio Aleni (1582–1649), whom he had come to know:

> Like rivers to the sea, one flows into the other.
> Mencius speaks of "serving Heaven";
> Sage Confucius speaks of "overcoming self."
> Who would think this man comes from a different country?
> The words he sets forth are of this very stripe!
> Geography? – What does it matter?
> What counts is that the frame of mind's the same.

It was this felt commonality that made Lang Shining's achievement possible. His work resonates with the view Maritain would express centuries later: Christian art is not limited to church-related things but extends to anything that is beautiful and spiritually radiant. As the apostle Paul enjoined in Philippians 4:8: "Whatever is true, whatever is honorable, whatever is just, whatever is pure, whatever is pleasing, whatever is commendable, if there is any excellence and if there is anything worthy of praise, think about these things."

Lang Shining's work is a guide for the Christian West into the world of Chinese painting, and so into the world of Chinese contemplation. The dialogue within his paintings between Chinese composition, framing, and vision and Italian perspective, depth, and shade echoes the spiritual dialogue that occurred when the Jesuits met with the Confucians in the court of the Kangxi Emperor. Lang Shining's paintings contain what both traditions share, and each has its own unique ways of revealing – that contemplation of nature which attempts to see and love things as they are, and to understand their spiritual meaning.

THE PHILOSOPHER JOSEF PIEPER said that contemplation consists of looking at something, anything, for its own sake, and saying "yes" to it. "Yes," you are good; you are lovely; it is good that you are here. Contemplative affirmation is ultimately grounded in a deeper affirmation, a "yes" to the world and to its source. It is an echo of the primeval utterance of God on his creation: "Indeed, it was very good" (Gen. 1:31).

"There is no nonreligious contemplation," Pieper wrote. "Awareness of the divine element can be kindled by virtually anything encountered." Prayer – praise – is incipient in the affirmation.

The minimalism of these paintings, the use of emptiness, the perspective of totality, the emotion of the brushwork – all are meant to reveal the poetry in things, the transcendent in nature. They help us to see earth as permeated by heaven. In this, the tenth-century painter Jing Hao rightly called them "divine."

Rainer Maria Rilke observed that when we look at the beautiful, it looks back into us. In the light of beauty, we understand that we must change our lives for the better. In drawing us into a contemplation that reaches out to God, the beauty of Chinese landscape paintings can help us overcome ourselves and to serve heaven. ≫

WESLEY HILL

Chaim Potok's Wandering Jews

Holding to Faith in a Critical Age

AT THE HEART OF CHAIM POTOK'S 1985 novel *Davita's Harp* is a child who is searching for faith. The parents of Ilana Davita Chandal offer little help. Her father was raised Christian in New England but has abandoned his earlier Evangelical fervor. Her mother, a Polish Jewish immigrant, has given up observance of the mitzvot and joined the Communist Party; she is now committed to fighting the fascism she hears is on the verge of consuming Western Europe. Through much of the book, Davita seems unsettled by the snatches of religious language and observance she is able to pick up. When her aunt urges her

Yoram Raanan, *Har Sinai Bavli*, oil on canvas and book cover collage, 2019 to have faith in Jesus, Davita raises the classic Jewish objection: "Why is there a war in Spain if Jesus is the Prince of Peace?" Later, when Davita finds her mother's King James Bible and takes it to synagogue, she horrifies her peers: "They all backed away a step or two as if I were holding in my hand a specimen of forbidden vermin." "That's a goyische Bible," her friend tells her, making her blush with shame. "I did not go back to that synagogue for a long time," Davita says.

Yet in 1937, she does return, after learning of her father's death in the bombing of Guernica, where he had been working as a journalist. It is one of the novel's pivotal scenes. Davita goes back to a synagogue and, finding herself in a kind of daze, says softly aloud the Kaddish, the traditional doxology that asks for the sanctification of God's name. Davita mouths the words in memory of her father. She can see the men's side of the synagogue through the curtain. She watches the men rise.

And then I was on my feet too, listening to the voices on the other side of the curtain and reciting faintly with the men the words of the Kaddish, which I found, to my astonishment, that I knew by heart. There was a surge of whispering, a soft surflike rush of sound from the women around me. Someone said, "What is she doing?" Another said something in Yiddish. I stood, quietly reciting the words. There has to be more for you, Papa, than just one memorial service. Can one recite the Kaddish for a father who wasn't a Jew? I didn't care. I went on. The Kaddish ended. I sat down and closed my eyes, feeling upon my face the hot stares of all those nearby.

The service went on. Then, moments later, I heard again the words of the Kaddish, and I rose and began to recite them too, louder this

time, and I thought I heard one or two of the women answer, "Amen."

Maybe it is because I think about Paul Ricoeur's diagnosis of modern readers of the Bible and would-be believers in its God – "Beyond the desert of criticism, we wish to be called again" – that I am tempted to regard Davita's budding curiosity about Judaism as one of the most immediately relatable entries into Chaim Potok's work as a whole. A religiously observant life is less and less accessible or intelligible to modern Westerners, yet many of us remain haunted by its possibility. Even the demographic designation "nones" invokes religious sensibility by naming its absence, tacitly acknowledging that, even in the desert, faith's echo can be heard. Davita's halting entry into an observant life dramatizes a journey we too might take. Her story makes the prospect of finding a home within a religious tradition, even in a secular age, a live, beguiling one.

HERMAN HAROLD POTOK WAS BORN on the eve of the Depression in the Bronx. The son of distinguished Hasidic parents, Chaim – as he was known at home and later in the world of literature – grew up in a devout and strictly observant Jewish community. He attended the more liberal Yeshiva University's boys' high school and later the university itself in New York and was ordained to the (even more liberal, by the standards of his childhood) Conservative rabbinate after training for four years at the Jewish Theological Seminary, also in New York. Eventually he earned a doctorate in philosophy at the University of Pennsylvania, in order, he said,

---

Wesley Hill is associate professor of biblical studies at Trinity School for Ministry. His most recent book is The Lord's Prayer: A Guide to Praying to Our Father *(Lexham, 2019). A contributing editor for* Comment *magazine, he writes regularly for* Christianity Today *and* Living Church.

"to see what the center of the Western World was really like." He started writing fiction in high school, despite the fact that his fellow Hasidim regarded it "at best as a frivolity, and at worst as a menace," as he would later put it. Talmudic scholarship was an admirable aim for a Jewish boy of Potok's world; becoming a writer of stories was not.

Potok published his first novel in 1967, when he was thirty-eight years old. *The Chosen* spent over six months on the *New York Times* bestseller list and was a finalist for the National Book Award. Like its eventual successor *Davita's Harp*, *The Chosen* is chiefly interested in what an observant Jewish life might look like in a modern Western context, but it comes at the matter from the other direction. Where Davita tiptoes her way into shul attendance and the study of Talmud, the protagonists of *The Chosen* can't remember a time when they weren't immersed the world of Judaism. For them, the question isn't about how to be at home in a forbiddingly strict and insular realm of piety but about how to embody their devotion to it within a wider secular culture that has little use for it – and how to allow that world's ideals to challenge the way they practice their Judaism, too.

In *The Chosen*, Danny Saunders is the son of his tight-knit Brooklyn community's formidable rebbe, which in the Hasidic tradition means he is also his father's designated successor. In high school, however, he secretly studies Sigmund Freud and yearns for graduate studies in psychology. The tension between his Hasidic identity and his apparent destiny on the one hand, and his burgeoning thirst for secular learning on the other, is unrelieved throughout most of the novel. At the climax, we see Danny refuse the choice: he will go on to become a psychologist, studying among the goyim, but he will remain an observer of the

commandments, albeit not as a rabbi.

The same tension animates all of Potok's best novels. In his second, *The Promise*, Reuven Malter is studying at an Orthodox rabbinical school under the watchful and forbidding ministrations of Rav Kalman, a Holocaust survivor who views Reuven's father's secular Zionism and historical-critical interpretations of the Talmud with suspicion and fear, and who watches for, and prepares to stifle, signs of their influence on Reuven. As Reuven begins to prepare for his ordination exams, Rav Kalman urges him away from modern

A religiously observant life is less and less accessible to modern Westerners, yet many of us remain haunted by its possibility.

critical approaches to the sacred page. One of the novel's most thrilling scenes is Reuven's oral examination. For anyone who has studied Jewish or Christian scripture in their original Hebrew and Greek, and who has pored over commentaries on both, as I have, it is hard to overstate how well Potok manages to evoke the tingling excitement a student can experience when performing a close reading of a text. At one point during Reuven's examination Rav Kalman draws his attention to a passage from the Mishnah, the second-century CE collection of the so-called "Oral Torah," part of the rabbinic tradition of Talmudic interpretation. Here is how Reuven, called upon to explain the passage, describes the scene:

> It was one of the passages I had been waiting for. There were others like it scattered all through the Talmud. Sooner or later I would have managed to steer us onto one, or we would have come across one by ourselves. Now I was in it and explaining it and knowing exactly what words I would use and seeing it all half a dozen steps in advance like a chess game.

Potok's best novels probe what it means to "hold" to tradition in a new, changed way.

The scene climaxes with Reuven's rabbinical examiners listening open-mouthed as Reuven demonstrates his mastery of the Talmud as well as of modern critical approaches to its study, even as he declares that he will remain an observant Jew and protect the sanctity of the Pentateuch as divinely given.

In the Beginning, published six years after *The Promise*, goes even further into the territory of modern critical study. Its protagonist, David Lurie, a yeshiva student, tells his father that not only does he want to know about modern critical approaches to Talmud, he also wants to see how secular university researchers and lecturers apply them to scripture itself. His father responds, "Tell me what it means to study Bible in a university. Your teachers will be goyim?" David says there will be Jews at the university too, though not all will be observant. "How can a goy who believes in Jesus or in nothing teach a Jew the Torah? How can a sinful Jew teach the Torah?" his father retorts. But David, like Reuven Malter, refuses to accept his father's presumption that critical study of the Bible and an observant Jewish life must necessarily be in conflict. In a moving moment, one generous rabbi offers private encouragement to David not to shy back from the university but to bring the fruits of his learning back to his Orthodox community afterwards:

> Lurie, if the Torah cannot go out into your world of scholarship and return stronger, then we are all fools and charlatans. I have faith in the Torah. I am not afraid of truth. . . . I want to know if the religious world view has any meaning today. Bring yourself back an answer to that, Lurie. Take apart the Bible and see if it is something more today than the *Iliad* and the *Odyssey*. Bring yourself back that answer, Lurie.

In what is for me Potok's most disturbingly powerful achievement of all, his third novel, *My Name Is Asher Lev*, we meet another young Brooklyn Hasid, the son of inspiringly just and devout parents, this one with a gift for art. Through his adolescence, Asher Lev devotes all his attention to drawing and painting, to the bafflement and then to the hurt and angry bewilderment of his family and wider Orthodox community. Several years later, after he gains notoriety as an artist, Asher is driven to try to depict the pain he had watched on his mother's face as she parented him alone while his father traveled the world at the rebbe's request, rescuing persecuted Jews.

Asher had watched her standing in pain astride the gap between her devout, traditionalist husband and the defiant son who could never understand – or be understood by – his father. What other symbol could possibly suffice for this depiction, Asher asks himself, than the form of the cross, the same symbol under which the Jews his father spent his life rescuing were driven from their homes and killed in pogroms? When Asher's parents attend his show at a prominent New York gallery, Asher watches in agony as his father glimpses his final two paintings, *Brooklyn Crucifixion I* and *II*, in which his mother occupies the center, "tied to the vertical and horizontal lines."

> Then my father moved toward the paintings. I saw him bend to read the titles. His shoulders stiffened. Then he saw the name of the museum that had purchased the paintings. He straightened slowly. He turned and looked at me. His face wore an expression of awe and rage and bewilderment and sadness, all at the same time. . . . Who are you? the expression said. Are you really my son? . . . He did not speak to me.

Like Potok's characters Danny Saunders and David Lurie, Asher Lev is compelled to venture beyond the confines of his father's carefully circumscribed world, but he does so without abandoning his Judaism. He cannot be a Hasid, but he chooses to remain an observer of the commandments.

One of Potok's sharpest and most sympathetic critics, Daniel Walden, founder of the Jewish Studies Program at Penn State, says that every Potok novel always circles around two basic questions: "1) how to live as an observant Jew in a secular society, and 2) to what degree [one can] hold to the tradition of Orthodox separateness in a secular society." I think that is true as far as it goes, but Potok's best novels

(with *Davita's Harp* the exception, as I earlier hinted) probe what it *means* to "hold" to tradition in a new, changed way. Potok's Hasidic protagonists never give up Jewish observance, but they do, all of them, practice their Judaism in a way that represents a genuine break with their past understandings and practices of it. The Hebrew Bible scholar Jon Levenson, from his perspective as an observant Jew who teaches at Harvard, has remarked on the ability of some religious scholars, Jews and Christians alike, to hold together their use of modern critical biblical studies with an ongoing faith in their inherited religious traditions. In this way, Levenson says, using Ricoeur's phrase, "the 'second naiveté' of those touched by historical criticism is to be distinguished from the innocence of the orthodox believer who has never become aware of the historical context and who does not feel the claim of historical investigation." The novels of Chaim Potok dramatize young Jews finding their way to forms of Jewish life they wish to hold on to – their "second naiveté" – but at the real cost of leaving behind their former innocence and shocking or even alienating their communities of origin in the process.

IT IS THIS ASPECT OF POTOK'S WORK – his portrayal of young religious fundamentalists who are confronting modernity and negotiating their tradition in the process – that I think explains my initial enthrallment with his novels when I discovered them in my early twenties. There was, at first, a shock of recognition: I, a Gentile and an Evangelical Christian, knew something of what it was like to grow up in Potok's world. The theorist and professor Michael Warner has spoken of the Pentecostal church culture of his childhood as a "profoundly hermeneutic" one:

"Where I come from, people lose sleep over the meanings of certain Greek and Hebrew words. . . . Being a literary critic is nice, I have to say, but for lip-whitening, vein-popping thrills it doesn't compete. Not even in the headier regions of Theory can we approximate that saturation of life by argument" – by ongoing contestation, that is, of the sentences and paragraphs of Scripture.

That captures my childhood church and family culture too, perfectly, and to this day I haven't lost the conviction that when one is reading the Bible, the stakes are high. The agonies and desperations of Potok's characters are instantly recognizable to me. ("Even though the faith Potok writes of is orthodox or Hasidic Judaism, Evangelical readers [and there are many] find themselves understanding and empathizing with the conflicts he presents," wrote Cheryl Forbes in *Christianity Today* in 1978.)

I was also drawn to the extraordinary depictions of friendship between young men in Potok. Daniel Walden says that the friendship Danny Saunders and Reuven Malter enjoy in *The Chosen* is "a kind of love story," which I take to be a clumsy effort to sum up the way their relationship isn't romantic and yet is obviously much more intimate than what one often encounters in similar portrayals – or in real life, for that matter. Daniel Boyarin, professor of Talmudic cultures at Berkeley, has made the case that "Judaism provides exempla for another kind of masculinity, one in which men do not manifest 'a deeply rooted concern about the possible meanings of dependence on other males.'" Potok's novels themselves provide some of these exempla, as their male characters confide their secrets in one another, confess to each other their insecurities and ambitions, and at times weep with or in front

of each other. In my post-college years of loneliness, angst, and longing for male friendship, I found this aspect of Potok's novels almost unbearably poignant.

But their primary source of power for me comes from their dramatization of the quest to retain one's childhood faith in a new, altered form. I recall taking courses in the Hebrew text of the Old Testament and the Greek text of the New Testament at a conservative Christian college and learning, for the first time, about biblical criticism. I learned about what textual critics call variants – differences in wording and syntax of biblical verses that appear in various extant manuscripts, forcing translators to choose which ones they think are best supported over others they find less likely to be original. I was forced to grapple with tensions within the canonical texts that I had never noticed before. Mark 10:46, for example, says: "And as he [Jesus] was leaving Jericho with his disciples and a great crowd, Bartimaeus, a blind beggar, was sitting by the roadside." But in Luke's version (18:35), Jesus notices the blind beggar as he *arrives* at Jericho. Matthew's Gospel has Judas committing suicide by hanging (27:3–10), whereas the Book of Acts has him die by falling and gashing his abdomen open (1:18–19). What, I wondered, did tensions like this mean for belief in the Bible's inerrancy – its status of being inspired, without falsehood in matters of doctrine as well as historically and scientifically accurate? Reading Potok, I met characters who lost sleep over questions like this too.

I read a lot these days about "exvangelicals" – people who had upbringings like mine who now want nothing to do with them, people who have left Evangelical Christianity behind for good, owing variously to its anti-intellectual impulses; its demand for cultural and political conformity; its tribal disdain for those deemed outsiders; its inability to self-criticize, with sometimes abusive results; or all of the above. I understand and sympathize with the "exvangelicals." In many ways, I am one. Like Potok's characters, I went away to university and experienced something of the wider world beyond the confines of my Baptist, Republican childhood. I now make use of historical critical tools in my biblical scholarship and seminary classroom, and I am now a member of the Episcopal Church, which, to my childhood eyes, was barely a church at all.

Even so, the Evangelical faith in which I was nurtured continues to beguile, inspire, and compel me in ways I am still discovering. I can't be the Christian I used to be, but I want still, very much, to be a Christian. Potok's characters help me understand my complicated feelings. They are not only interested in the deconstructive moment, in which childhood certainties are relinquished. They strive also for the chastened second naiveté, on the far side of the desert of criticism, that will make it possible for them to go on being faithfully Jewish.

The eighteenth-century aphorist G. C. Lichtenberg says there is "a great difference between believing something *still* and believing it *again*." The novels of Chaim Potok show us what the latter looks like, and in doing so, make believers like me feel much less alone.

In 1976, after the publication of *In the Beginning*, Potok talked with interviewer Harold Ribalow. Ribalow asked, "Why do you think non-Jews read your books?" Potok replied:

> What non-Jews are doing – if I can get it from the letters they are sending me – is that they are simply translating themselves into the particular context of the boys and the fathers and the mothers and the situation that I'm

writing about. So instead of being a Jew, you are a Baptist; instead of being an Orthodox Jew, you are a Catholic; and the dynamic is the *same*. The particular words or expressions that might be used might be Jewish or what have you, but they are simply putting themselves in the place of the subculture which is clashing core to core with the umbrella culture in which we all live.

It is no accident, probably, that Potok mentions Baptists and Catholics as the closest kin to the characters in his novels. "The Hebrew Torah is," according to Gerald Bruns, "a monumental

I can't be the Christian I used to be, but I want still, very much, to be a Christian.

example of a binding text; its significance lies not only in what it contains or means but also in its power over those who stand within its jurisdiction." Just this is the situation of those Christians – like the Baptists I grew up among – whose Bible exercises supreme authority in their traditions. For any readers, then, who treat Scripture as a "binding text," for any so-called "people of the Book," who, by dint of historical time and circumstance, must live with others who are not so bound and who marshal weighty arguments for their freedom, the novels of Chaim Potok will go on providing guidance and solace. ❧

KAREN SWALLOW PRIOR

How to Read Dickens

This October, Plough *is releasing* The Gospel in Dickens, *a new anthology edited by Gina Dalfonzo. From Karen Swallow Prior's foreword to the book:*

GOOD LITERATURE IS FRESH WATER for the soul. While some writers offer a sip ladled from the well, Dickens takes us to a mountain waterfall where rushing waters saturate, overwhelm, and put us at risk of drowning as we drink. But fear not. This book of selected readings is more like a gentle brook whose waters will quench the thirst of Dickens aficionados and neophytes alike. I know this volume will attract those who know and love Dickens already, but I hope it woos those who have yet to drink from his depths.

Dickens was, perhaps, the first real, grown-up, *literary* author I fell in love with. I think that happened because I was allowed to wade into the stream gradually when I was first assigned *Great Expectations* by my junior-high English teacher. By using an abridged, illustrated version for young readers, my teacher introduced us to the storytelling powers of Dickens without letting us get lost in the baroque style that is beyond the tastes and abilities of inexperienced readers. The images from that early immersion in an

Karen Swallow Prior is Research Professor of English and Christianity and Culture at Southeastern Baptist Theological Seminary and is the author of On Reading Well: Finding the Good Life through Great Literature *(Brazos, 2018).* Plough.com/GospelinDickens.

age-appropriate version have remained with me my whole life, deepened and enriched with each rereading. The memories of the eccentric Miss Havisham, her decaying cake crawling with spiders, the sparring of the mysterious Pale Young Gentleman, and of course, the alternatingly endearing and annoying Pip are as vivid in my mind as memories of real-life people and events.

I was lucky enough to have a teacher who helped me develop that taste, not only for Dickens but for all of the demands that good literature makes upon readers. The difference between a great book and one written (and read) merely to entertain or pass the time is that good literature demands an investment from the reader in order to reap its rewards. Reading good literature well doesn't always come easily. Sometimes the challenge of literary art presents itself in its otherness (being by or about people from times and places vastly different from ours). Almost always the challenge comes from the artful use of language – words sparer, richer, less direct, or more resonant than those we use in everyday speech.

Both of these challenges – otherness and artfulness – are present in Dickens for today's readers. Dickens's style is difficult for those of us habituated to the plain, flat prose of cable news, blog posts, Twitter feeds, or Ernest Hemingway. To read Dickens well, not only for newcomers but even for me, a seasoned reader, requires deliberately arming ourselves against our usual hurry and our shortening attention spans. Readers of Dickens need to be willing to slow their reading pace, luxuriate in the circumlocutory sentences, reread passages that take unexpected turns, and tune their ear to the cadence of the multiple voices that inhabit Dickens's busy, busy world. Whether the massive *Bleak House* or the short but

still demanding *A Christmas Carol*, Dickens requires a commitment of time, attention, effort, and patience.

But that commitment is well worth it. For even beyond the literary merits of his works, Dickens puts forth, as Gina Dalfonzo explains in the introduction, a profoundly Christian view of the world. And while the redemptive elements are some of the strongest within the body of his work, perhaps what can speak most powerfully to our world today is the theme of guilt. Dickens is prophetic in the way he illuminates the distinctions we of a modern, increasingly secular world often fail to make between real guilt and false shame, between true repentance and cheap substitutions. More and more today – as in the world of these novels – the truly guilty feel no shame, those who feel greatly ashamed are the most innocent, and those who say they're sorry don't have the godly sorrow that brings repentance.

To read Dickens requires arming ourselves against our usual hurry and our shortening attention spans.

Thus, the division of the excerpts from Dickens's work into sections on sin, repentance, and righteousness is true not only to Dickens's major concerns but to ones we ought to have today as well. While this volume is a curated selection, this arrangement and the introduction offer a picture of Dickens's entire corpus. To return to my opening metaphor, the wide-ranging, insightfully arranged selections here encourage those whose souls thirst for more to follow the exhortation of Alexander Pope, a poet who lived a century before Dickens:

Drink deep, or taste not the Pierian spring:
There shallow draughts intoxicate the brain,
And drinking largely sobers us again. ➤

Opposite: Charles Dickens, 1863

ANTJE VOLLMER

A Communal Publishing House

The Founding of Plough – and of the Bruderhof

This year both Plough Publishing House and the Bruderhof communities mark the hundredth anniversary of their founding. Both had their origin in Neuwerk (New Work), a Christian socialist youth movement in Germany after World War I in which Eberhard Arnold, Plough's founding editor, was a leading figure. Vollmer, author of a 2016 book on Neuwerk, tells the story in this adapted excerpt.

IN THE SPRING OF 2014, I received a surprising phone call. One hundred years after the outbreak of the First World War, a pastors' conference of the Protestant Church in Hesse and Nassau was reflecting on the war's consequences for their region and came across my doctoral thesis. I was astonished: forty-one years had passed since the writing of this dissertation and it had never appeared in print. At that time, my doctoral supervisors Helmut

---

Antje Vollmer is a Protestant pastor and a politician in Germany's Green Party. From 1994 to 2005 she was vice president of the nation's parliament.

Gollwitzer and Karl Kupisch suggested that I investigate one of the most interesting groups among the youth movements that emerged from the catastrophes of the First World War, whose members had exercised significant influence on the International Fellowship of Reconciliation, religious socialism, and the Confessing Church. This research was now all part of my distant past. Historians researching individual members or the movement as a whole had occasionally asked me for my dissertation to use as a source, but I did not want to give away my last personal copy. How could a Hessian pastors' conference even know of it?

It turned out that, in 2002, some members of the group whose beginnings I had researched had returned to the house in Germany where their movement started, after all kinds of odysseys – expulsion by the National Socialists in 1937, a stopover in England, building of new settlements in Paraguay, and a temporary union with the Hutterite Brethren. Now they were again in the same Sannerz villa where everything began in 1920 when Eberhard Arnold moved in: the first Pentecost meetings with up to a thousand young participants, the first communal Bruderhof settlement, the creation and distribution of their own progressive magazine.

Before that phone call I had not heard anything about their return and this new beginning. I wanted to experience this for myself and so, before going to the pastors' conference, I visited the refounded Bruderhof. There I met many young people who happened to be visiting and wanted to experience the roots of their community for themselves. I was surprised to hear these guests – coming from many countries – singing the old songs of the youth movement in the original German by heart and powerfully, as if one hundred years of complicated European history had not

intervened. In the end, no doubt remained: here was, still or again, the Bruderhof movement, at its beginning identical with the Neuwerk movement, which I had once treated as a historically completed process. Today it has about three thousand members worldwide.

In conventional Protestant church historiography, the Neuwerk movement has remained largely unknown over the past century, although its circle and its published writings included such prominent personalities as the theologians Karl Barth and Paul Tillich; the social philosopher Eugen Rosenstock-Huessy; the economist Eduard Heimann; the social worker Gertrud Staewen; and the Christian socialist Helmut Gollwitzer. This relegation to obscurity may seem surprising at first glance, but it is a fate that the Neuwerk movement shares with quite a number of progressive social movements from the short Weimar period between the world wars, including labor movement organizations, trade unions, nature

Opposite: At a 1920 Pentecost conference convened by Eberhard Arnold, a new movement was born.

Below: Postcard set designed by Otto Salomon, published by Neuwerk.

Eberhard Arnold *(center)* looking over a manuscript for typesetting

The main source of information about the history of the Neuwerk movement lies in the almost completely preserved fifteen volumes of the magazine *Das neue Werk (The New Work)*, which gave the movement its name and appeared between 1919 and 1935 with about five hundred closely printed pages per year. It reflects the lively discussion through which the members and protagonists of the Neuwerk movement tried to live up to the challenges of their time. This included examining the causes of World War I; orienting the youth movement in its own self-determination between nationalist and communist tendencies; exploring questions of pacifism and a just social order; and calling for communal settlements, worker education, progressive schools, and ongoing adult education.

The magazine also included precise descriptions of the social situation of workers and the unemployed in the large cities and analyses of the threats to democracy from the instability of the Weimar Republic and the world economic crisis. Especially in the early years, the language of many articles is remarkable: fresh, charismatic, rapturous, excited, polemical.

In retrospect, it seems to me that my early research in this area prepared me well for the language, themes, struggles, passions, life experiments, and characters that I met ten years later among the first Green Party members in the German parliament.

conservation and sports movements, women's associations, and many creative cultural groups. Some of them fell into oblivion because they were ultimately considered unsuccessful in the face of the rise of National Socialism, while others were denounced as conscious or unconscious forerunners of that era. This applied to many groups of the youth movement, whose culture and way of life were later almost completely appropriated by the Nazi youth associations, which sought to benefit from their undeniable charisma and attractiveness to young people. And yet it is worth a closer look to avoid over-hasty historical condemnations. What was imagined and hoped for in those hard years between the wars – what visions for a more just world were dreamed of, and what daring reform projects were undertaken – still deserves our unbiased interest.

THE BEGINNING OF NEUWERK would have been unthinkable without Eberhard Arnold. He managed, within a short time, to set so many young people all over Germany on fire for his cause that two to three hundred of them answered his invitation to a Pentecost conference in 1920 – the Neuwerk movement's hour of birth.

All who knew Eberhard Arnold speak of the extraordinary strength his person radiated, of his enthusiastic faith, which was the faith of Jesus' Sermon on the Mount, and of his radical way of carrying out the task he knew himself called to. H. J. Schoeps, a Jewish member of the German Youth Movement during the 1920s, describes him in his memoir:

> I remember a very tall man of about forty-five in corduroy clothes, with radiant brown eyes, which gazed down at you in a friendly but also challenging way. He looked unusual in every respect. Once when he was standing in front of the National Library in Berlin, curious Berliners formed a proper circle around him and just stared at him. . . . I state without hesitation that powers from another world were at work here, and Eberhard Arnold was their chosen instrument. If he had lived a few centuries earlier and as a Catholic, he would now most likely have a place assigned to him in a saints' calendar.

Before World War I, Eberhard and his wife Emmy had been leading figures in Germany's evangelical revival movement. Called up for military service when war broke out, he was discharged because of severe tuberculosis and took a job in Berlin as editor at a Christian publishing house.

The 1919 revolution confirmed the Arnolds' determination, which had grown during the war, to try to close the rift between a radically understood Christianity and the endeavor to socially revolutionize the world. From this time on there were open evenings in their Berlin townhouse, attended by up to a hundred young people at a time: anarchists as well as members of Christian youth associations, atheists and Quakers, proletarians and intellectuals. All of them were looking for a new meaning for human existence and for new forms of life that would strengthen peace and social justice. They read and discussed Tolstoy, Dostoyevsky, and, repeatedly, the Sermon on the Mount.

From 1919 to 1920, Arnold grew to believe more strongly that the new vision of a radical Christianity could not remain just a theory, but that it compelled him to give up his bourgeois existence in Berlin and search for new, original forms of living.

Shortly after the Pentecost conference, on June 21, 1920, the Arnolds took over a villa in the village of Sannerz in Hesse, to build up an intentional community there in the spirit of the Neuwerk movement. Describing his vision for his new "settlement," Eberhard wrote in a 1920 letter:

> The important thing is that our religious-social movement and our young people, freely moved by Christ as they are, feel the urge to work together and to live in community. We need a center out in the country for our life, where we offer hiking groups a good place to stay and where we can at the same time bring together different work groups for the purpose of productive work and of mutual exchange of goods. What we have in mind is a community of life that is to have a common table and be a community of work, of goods, and of faith.

The Neuwerk movement's magazine and publishing house are the predecessors of Plough's *magazine and book publishing. The Gestapo forcibly dissolved both the community and publishing house in 1937, but the "New Work" carried on in England, where the first issue of the renamed English-language magazine* The Plough *would appear in March 1938.* ➤

Abridged translation by Kim Comer of excerpts from Antje Vollmer, Die Neuwerkbewegung: Zwischen Jugendbewegung und religiösem Sozialismus *(Herder, 2016).*

Plough

at One Hundred Years

Our Original Mission Statement from 1920

EBERHARD ARNOLD

One hundred years ago, as Germany reeled from World War I and the revolution that followed it, Plough's founding editor Eberhard Arnold announced the launch of a new publishing house, then called Neuwerk, the "New Work" (see previous article). This mission statement, which still guides our work, appears here with an illustrated timeline to celebrate one century of publishing.

THE NEUWERK PUBLISHING HOUSE is a communal publishing enterprise. It exists not for the profit of one or more entrepreneurs, but instead as a community of common purpose that manifests and pursues its shared spirit and goals through all forms of publishing. The publishing house takes its name from its biweekly magazine *Das neue Werk: der Christ im Volksstaat* (*The New Work: The Christian in Democracy*).

Eberhard Arnold (1883–1935) was a German theologian and cofounder of the Bruderhof.

The mission of the magazine shows the way forward for the mission of the publishing house as a whole. This mission is to proclaim living renewal, to summon people to the deeds of the spirit of Christ, to spread the mind that was in Jesus in the national and social distress of the present day, to apply Christianity publicly, to testify to God's action in the history of our days. Though this task is not tied to a church, it is a religious task. It means penetrating down to the deepest life forces of Christianity and demonstrating that they are indispensable for solving the most urgent problems in contemporary culture.

Why We Publish

Humankind, just like each individual, needs a renewal arising from the depths of the spiritual world. For this, it is equally fruitless either to withdraw passively into the interiority of the soul, or to throw oneself into the outward exertion of moral effort or activist gesturing.

Rather, what matters is that an active life of deeds gains nourishment from the blessing of inwardness in God and the wholesomeness of the pure atmosphere of Christ. No advance in the education of the masses, no religious renewal, is possible without applying Christianity to every sphere of personal and public life. The practical efficacy of the highest spiritual powers must be proved in the world as it is: man must take a creative and formative role in the world, becoming the master, not the servant, of chaotic physical reality.

We need a publishing house that will encourage Christians to take up the tasks required today: to oppose all lust for war, all caste attitudes, all mammonism, by letting the spirit of Christ rule. We need a publishing house, accordingly, that is attentive to all actions and events that resist the forces of self-interest, hatred, and arrogance, one that musters every element of truth wherever it may be found – doing so from a perspective that

Opposite: A *Plough* logo design from 1940 by English typeface designer Eric Gill

1914

Dr. Arnold:
Vortragssaal Spielgartenstr. 43
Montag, 4. Dezember: **Befreiung des Einzelnen.**
Samstag, 4. Dezember. **Freiheit und Einheit.**
Eintritt frei! Beginn 8½ Uhr. *Eintritt frei!*

Eberhard Arnold, a young German theologian, is a nationally known lecturer. When war breaks out, he is soon discharged from military service due to tuberculosis and moves to Berlin to become editor of Furche, a Christian publishing house.

1915

During the war years, Arnold's experiences ministering to wounded soldiers and his growing awareness of class injustice cause him to question his patriotic Christianity and bourgeois lifestyle.

1919

Revolution sweeps through defeated Germany. Arnold and his wife, Emmy, hold weekly discussion evenings in their Berlin home *(above).* Inspired by the New Testament, they decide to found a communal settlement and a publishing house.

1920

With friends from the Christian socialist movement, Arnold founds the Neuwerk Publishing House, and moves with his family to a new communal settlement in the village of Sannerz. This marks the beginning of both Plough and the Bruderhof.

holds together the totality of the cosmos and world history.

A movement is springing up that places witness to Christ – Christ who was crucified, rose, and will come again – directly into the full context of life in a way that contemporary people, with their natural and newly awakened strong social conscience, look for and long for.

This presents Neuwerk with a double task. On the one hand, our task focuses on personal faith in Christ, that is, on the personal experience of faith and of practical action in the spirit of Christ; this involves putting ourselves on the side of the have-nots and working for justice against every injustice. It comes down to personal Christianity. From this focus emerges writing that highlights Christian faith, Christian love, and God's working in the Christian church.

On the other hand, our task focuses on God's working outside the Christian church, on the entirety of his action in human history and in the creation of the cosmos. Here our publishing house finds the second part of its task: to understand the divine significance of today's powerful movements advocating for the working class and for a peaceful future, recognizing how God is working toward his ultimate goal in the socialistic and pacifistic actualities of today. His goal is the future kingdom of peace and justice on earth; this is Christianity's hope. In view of this hope, our publishing house must stand for all those things in political and economic life, as well as in society's spiritual life, that strive for the goals of conscience belonging to this kingdom.

What We Publish

Among the many active publishing houses in our country, none has yet tackled these tasks. In contrast to many other social-minded publishing houses, for us it is decisive that activism in the service of love and the spirit of community must draw its strength from an

1920

Else von Hollander, Emmy's sister and Eberhard's assistant, is a cofounder of the community and becomes the business director of the publishing house.

1920

Neuwerk's magazine, which at first appears biweekly, publishes a heady mix of Christian, socialist, pacifist, and youth movement writers, including Leo Tolstoy, Karl Barth, Rosa Luxemburg, Martin Buber, and Christoph Blumhardt.

1921

Following the magazine's lead, Neuwerk's book program includes titles on both religion and social issues, such as Julius Goldstein's *Rasse und Politik*, a warning against German anti-Semitism.

1922

The Neuwerk movement splits between reformists and the radicals at Sannerz, and the publishing house is split up. Sannerz carries on the book publishing, but loses the magazine; starting in 1925, it publishes its own periodical.

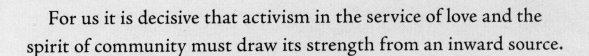

> For us it is decisive that activism in the service of love and the spirit of community must draw its strength from an inward source.

inward source. With this in mind, Neuwerk's *Inner Vision* series lets us hear the voices of people whose inner eye has caught a glimpse of the essence of things. Their affirmation of life is free of false narrowness (and free, too, from an overestimation of theological and philosophical modes of thinking); it looks out from the inner center to see what God is doing and thus what we should and must be doing. Figures such as Zinzendorf[1] and Landauer,[2] the

two Blumhardts,[3] and the Quakers guide us toward deeds born of the inner vision of faith.

But our concern is not a purely contemplative turn away from the outer world, and so the *Inner Vision* series does not stand on its own. Instead, it is the *New Work* series, which focuses broadly on economic, political, and social life, that actually represents our movement's program. In this series, we are concerned with God's history, with God's action in the entire context of humanity, with the future state that Jesus will bring, with the activism born of faith.

1. Count Nicolaus Zinzendorf (1700–1760), German religious and social reformer and bishop of the Moravian Brethren (*Unitas Fratrum*).
2. Gustav Landauer (1870–1919), social anarchist, pacifist, and Jewish mystic whose thought inspired community movements including the Bruderhof and kibbutzim. Landauer had been murdered by right-wing paramilitaries just months before this statement was written.
3. Johann Christoph Blumhardt (1805–1880), German Lutheran pastor and pioneer of kingdom-now theology. Christoph Friedrich Blumhardt (1842–1919), his son, was also a Lutheran pastor, evangelist, and founder of the Christian socialist movement to which Karl Barth, Eberhard Arnold, and the Neuwerk network belonged.

1933

In November 1933, ten months after Hitler's rise to power, the community and publishing house are raided by around 150 armed Gestapo and police, who confiscate letters, books with red covers ("Communist"), and art portfolios ("pornography").

1936

Facing increasing harassment by the Nazi regime, the publishing house hangs on – barely. In one case, book signatures are buried, then smuggled out of Germany in knapsacks. in 1936, the printing press is "sold" to friends in England for safekeeping.

1937

April 1937 brings another Gestapo raid; the publishing house and community are legally dissolved, their directors are imprisoned, and community members are ordered out of the country. They regroup in England, where the printing press awaits them.

1938

In the village of Ashton Keynes, the publishing house sets up shop as the Plough Publishing House, with a quarterly magazine *The Plough: Towards the Coming Order* and a book line aimed at the British and European peace movement.

Then, still from the viewpoint of religious inwardness, the *Homeland* series allows us to view the realm of nature, which discloses to us the whole of created life as coming from Christ and leading to Christ. In this series, the eye illumined by God looks at life and at nature as given by God, recognizing in it the best connecting point for every naturally sensitive person to the highest and ultimate values.

The connections that come to expression in these books are not dependent on the arbitrary decisions of an editor or group of authors. Rather, they arise from a growing and developing movement. This movement expresses itself in our publishing house's anthologies: *The Plough* (1920) is a collection of mature authors, both men and women, who are active in the movement and represent the most varied points of view within it. *Fresh Seed* is dedicated to the Youth Movement, a movement that is led and motivated by the same powers as our own; in this book, Youth Movement participants show how the divine seed is at work everywhere.

What Guides Us

Today a movement is arising, both within student groups and among working-class youth, which can only be termed *Christian* and *social* in the sense used here. This movement strives toward the personal and the inward, toward the immediate and the absolute; it is intensely conscious of the experience of nature and of the developing international solidarity of all humankind.

Here in Germany several revolutionary youth groups are embracing this spirit, and many Christian youth circles that until now were caged in dogmatic and political narrowmindedness are now awakening to this deep liberation of the soul. Meanwhile, within the romantic-tinged movement of the Free German Youth and the circles allied with it there are both smaller and larger groups who long for a decisive experience of Christ. Likewise, in the communal settlement movement there is a deepening realization that only

1940s

In 1940, the British government tells the Bruderhof to emigrate or face internment of its German nationals. Most of the community moves to the jungles of Paraguay; a handful remains in England and publishes occasional Plough booklets and brochures.

1950s

Plough's magazine is published in Spanish from Uruguay as *El Arado*. In 1950 in England, the Wheathill Bruderhof resumes publishing books and *The Plough* periodical, which at one point appears in eleven languages including Esperanto.

1960s

In 1963, Plough's headquarters moves from England to the United States. The magazine lapses, while book production is built out in Pennsylvania and New York, staffed largely by young men doing alternative service as conscientious objectors to the Vietnam War.

1970s

Plough publishes one or more books per year as well as numerous pamphlets. Hand typesetting, printing, and binding are all done in-house. Top titles include *Children in Community* (a photo essay) and *Behold That Star* (a Christmas story anthology).

the renewing spirit of original Christianity can achieve the communal form of life and education which so many have (unsuccessfully) tried to establish.

It is Neuwerk's task to allow all these various influences, guided by the right Spirit, to work on the people of our German nation. Germany's sacred mission – to be a people of inwardness and of actions that flow from inwardness – is in reality not Germany's alone, but rather corresponds to the deepest and most fundamental vocation of all humanity. Thus, our publishing house affirms that it belongs in its goals and development to the Christian international workers' movement [*Christliche Internationale*], which in many countries around the world seeks and professes this new way of life guided by the action of God's love.

With breadth of vision and energetic daring, our publishing house must steer its course right into the torrent of contemporary thought. Its work in fields that are apparently religiously neutral will lead to new relationships that open new doors for our life's most important tasks.

It is therefore also important for us that the production of our books meets the requirements of the best artistic taste. We must avoid anything affected or strained. Simplicity and genuineness should mark our work; here lies the secret of what is beautiful and true.

Abridged translation by Eileen Robertshaw and Peter Mommsen from Eberhard Arnold, "Der Neuwerk Verlag" (Bruderhof Historical Archive, EA 20/32). Headings added for clarity.

1990s

2000s

2010s

1980s

In 1983, *The Plough* resumes quarterly publication, profiling figures from Vincent Harding to César Chávez. Focuses include Anabaptism, building a culture of life, and abolishing the death penalty.

Plough's coverage broadens dramatically. A Columbine shooting memoir hits bestseller lists; a Darryl Strawberry memoir flops. Books by Bruderhof pastor Johann Christoph Arnold, praised by Mother Teresa and Nelson Mandela, anchor the booklist.

The Breaking the Cycle program, based on J. C. Arnold's *Why Forgive?*, reaches tens of thousands of middle school and high school students, especially after 9/11. In 2003, Plough shifts from print to digital publishing; the Daily Dig email newsletter gains 190,000 subscribers.

In 2013, Plough restarts its book program, with 8–10 English titles per year. Additional languages include Spanish, German, Korean, Arabic, and French. In 2014, *Plough Quarterly* relaunches. By 2020, the print magazine has 15,000 subscribers, with 5 million online visitors annually.

NEW RELEASE

Another Life Is Possible
Insights from 100 Years of Life Together

Created by Clare Stober; Photographs by Danny Burrows; Foreword by Rowan Williams

This Humans of New York–style book on lived Christian socialism includes profiles of one hundred members of the Bruderhof, past and present, and encompasses themes of technology, education, and sharing everything.

Hardcover, 320 pages, $40.00
anotherlifeispossible.com

No Lasting Home
A Year in the Paraguayan Wilderness

Emmy Barth; Foreword by Alfred Neufeld

As Hitler's armies turn mainland Europe into a mass graveyard, a little group of three hundred pacifist refugees – half of them babies and young children – looks for a new home. Where should the refugees try to resettle next? This is one year of their story.

Softcover, 214 pages, $12.00

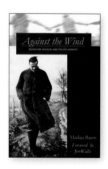

Against the Wind
Eberhard Arnold and the Bruderhof

Markus Baum; Foreword by Jim Wallis

A journalist's biography of Eberhard Arnold, a man who, in his search for Christ, ended up turning the Christianity of his day on its head. Markus Baum looks at the forces that shaped Arnold's life, recreates the colorful era in which he lived, and shows Arnold's connection with his contemporaries.

Thich Nhat Hanh, author, *Love in Action*:
Arnold's life is a testimony that in community the Spirit, which can be found in all traditions, can reveal to us the real causes of social injustice.

Softcover, 310 pages, $18.00

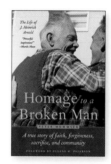

Homage to a Broken Man
The Life of J. Heinrich Arnold – A true story of faith, forgiveness, sacrifice, and community

Peter Mommsen; Foreword by Eugene Peterson

Those who knew J. Heinrich Arnold later in life wondered at the way people were drawn to this strange man with a thick accent and easy smile. In his presence, complete strangers poured out their darkest secrets and left transformed. Others wanted him dead.

Gold Medal Winner, Independent Publisher Book Awards

Robert Ellsberg, Editor-in-Chief, Orbis Books:
This inspiring biography does more than simply recount the story of a fascinating life. It describes an adventure that challenges the reader to ask, "What would my life look like if I lived as if the Gospel were really true?"

Hardcover, 415 pages, $22.00

All books 40% off for *Plough Quarterly* subscribers. Use code PQ40 at checkout.

The God Who Heals
Words of Hope for a
Time of Sickness

*Johann Christoph
Blumhardt and Christoph
Friedrich Blumhardt;
Foreword by Rick Warren*

This collection of daily
biblical reflections will encourage anyone
facing sickness or an uncertain future.

Gold Medal Winner, Illumination Book Awards

Rick Warren: Whatever circumstance you are
facing right now, this book of daily readings will
help you focus on a closer relationship with Jesus,
our one true spiritual healer. Soak in these words
of hope by the Blumhardts and find healing
strength for your soul.

Hardcover, 208 pages, $18.00

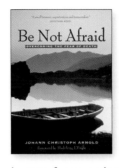

Be Not Afraid
Overcoming the Fear
of Death

*Johann Christoph Arnold;
Foreword by Madeleine
L'Engle*

This best-selling volume
addresses fears every
human faces – vulnerability, illness, aging, and
dying. Arnold says living for a cause greater
than ourselves enables us to face eternity
with the strength that comes from faith.

**Paul Brand, MD, author, *Pain: The Gift Nobody
Wants:*** I have read many books about dying,
but this is the one I would give to someone
approaching death or facing bereavement. From
start to finish it shines with hope.

Softcover, 222 pages, $12.00

If My Moon Was
Your Sun

*Andreas Steinhöfel;
Illustrated by Nele Palmtag;
Music by Bizet and
Prokofiev*

Did you hear about
the boy who kidnapped his grandpa from
a nursing home? This delightful tale helps
children talk about Alzheimer's and losing a
grandparent.

***School Library Journal,* starred review:** With its
loving portrayal of aging, caring for the elderly,
and the keen nature of kids' sensibilities, this is a
must-purchase for all libraries serving children.

Hardcover, 80 pages, $19.00 with a CD

Perfectly Human
Nine Months with Cerian

Sarah C. Williams

She knew they would
only have a few fleeting
months together, but in
that time Sarah's unborn
daughter would trans-
form her understanding of beauty, worth, and
the gift of life.

CT Women Book of the Year

Christianity Today: This is an important word for
those of us wrestling with suffering and struggling
for hope.

Softcover, 160 pages, $16.00

NEW RELEASE

The Gospel in Dickens
Selections from His Works

Edited by Gina Dalfonzo; Foreword by Karen Swallow Prior

Wish you had time to re-read and enjoy that daunting stack of Charles Dickens novels? Take heart: Dickens enthusiast Gina Dalfonzo has done the heavy lifting for you.

Softcover, 245 pages, $18.00

Home for Christmas
Stories for Young and Old

Elizabeth Goudge, Ernst Wiechert, George Sumner Albee, Madeleine L'Engle, Nikolai S. Lesskov, Pearl S. Buck, Henry van Dyke, Ruth Sawyer, Selma Lagerlöf, and others;

Compiled by Miriam LeBlanc; Illustrated by David Klein

Home for Christmas includes tales by some of the world's most beloved children's authors as well as little-known European stories not available in English anywhere else.

Jim Trelease, author, *The Read-Aloud Handbook:* If you're giving one book for Christmas, make it this one.

Softcover, 339 pages, $18.00

Watch for the Light
Readings for Advent and Christmas

Dorothy Day, C. S. Lewis, Oscar Romero, Philip Yancey, Dietrich Bonhoeffer, Alfred Delp, Søren Kierkegaard, Annie Dillard, Kathleen Norris, and others

Selections from the world's greatest spiritual writers provide inspiration for Advent and Christmas.

Publishers Weekly: It's hard to go wrong with writers such as these.... Born of obvious passion and graced with superb writing, this collection is a welcome – even necessary – addition.

Hardcover, 344 pages, $24.00

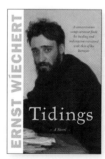

Tidings
A Novel

Ernst Wiechert

A concentration camp survivor, returning home to pick up the shards of his shattered life, finds his own healing and redemption inextricably entwined with that of his betrayer. Rediscover this classic in the tradition of Dostoyevsky and Tolstoy.

Time Magazine: One of the last of a vanished breed of German writers – romantic in feeling, mystical in outlook, spendthrift in prose.... Wiechert presses home his message with intense sincerity.

Hardcover, 360 pages, $24.00

All books 40% off for *Plough Quarterly* subscribers. Use code PQ40 at checkout.

(continued from page 112)

Image public domain

This joint household – full of children, because Macrina had the habit of adopting babies abandoned during times of famine – was a hub of theological conversation and a stable home for the brothers between travels.

It was not simply a center of intellectual ferment and political strategizing but a social experiment: Macrina had decided, as the community was forming, that there would be no distinctions in rank among its members. Some of the sisters, the women whose work she shared, had been her maid-servants; some of the brothers whose theological debate flowed freely at Basil and Peter's table had been born slaves.

They talked and they wrote, this family; they wrote a lot. They wrote about the kinds of things we write about, and read about: the Trinity, economics, the nature of justice, politics, the nuts and bolts of founding not just monasteries but monasti-cism itself. They wrote about each other too – Gregory wrote his sister's biog-raphy in the form of a letter to a monk called Olympius.

When Basil died, Gregory came to Macrina for comfort, only to find her also very ill. "Well, she gave in to me for a little while, like a skillful driver, in the ungovernable violence of my grief," he said, "and then she tried to check me by speaking, and to correct with the curb of her reasonings the disorder of my soul. She quoted the Apostle's words about the duty of not being *grieved for them that sleep*; because only *men without hope* have such feelings."

"Thou, O Lord, hast freed us from the fear of death."

Saint Macrina

He was not having it. "How can that ever be practiced by mankind? There is such an instinctive and deep-seated abhorrence of death in all!" Especially, he says, the death of those we love, those who made such good use of every moment, who had been so vividly alive.

She reminded him of the doctrine: the soul does not die; there is a resurrection. "But" – I'm paraphrasing – "how can I know? The Stoics say –" and they were off again, the two of them, debating. Once again she taught him: that day, the day before she died, she argued him into the ground, turning his eyes back to the God she would soon meet. She died with a prayer on her lips: "Thou, O Lord, hast freed us from the fear of death. Thou hast made the end of this life the beginning to us of true life . . ."

"Her life was such," Gregory wrote of the sister he called the Teacher, "since God provided for her, that she never stopped working her hands in the service of God neither did she turn away people who sought her help . . . for God with his blessings secretly made the small resources from her good works grow like seeds into an abundant stream of fruitfulness."

There's a hospitality in the accounts they left of each other, this astonishing family, like the hospitality that will be the great table-conversation of the kingdom, the talk flowing on, welcoming the guest and wayfarer with delight. ➤

Saint Macrina

SUSANNAH BLACK

With Artwork by Jason Landsel

AROUND AD 375, a Roman soldier and his wife visited a villa on the River Iris, in Turkey. They brought their baby daughter, who was suffering from an eye infection. The mistress of the villa, Macrina, cuddling the baby on her lap, noticed, and promised the couple an ointment that would cure it. They had dinner; the talk, which, the husband said, "entertained and cheered me royally," flowed freely, running to theology.

As the couple was heading home, the wife realized they'd forgotten the ointment. Irritated, the soldier told one of their servants to head back to Macrina's villa for it. But just then, his daughter, in her nurse's arms, looked over at her mother. The mother gasped. "Look! The healing which comes from prayer, she has given us; . . . there's nothing whatsoever left of the eye disease!" She took the baby from the nurse and put her in her father's arms. He looked, and all signs of infection were gone.

He hadn't, he said, believed in the miracles recorded in the Gospels. He did now. If God could do this through the prayers of this woman, then he could do the same in Christ, who healed the blind.

It is not the only such story told about Macrina, but it's an illustrative one. The eldest of nine surviving children, she was – by her brothers' accounts – the heart of the family, as well as its keenest mind; the one who taught them all, the one who drew them all, through her sheer delight in Christ, to lives that shook the world.

Two of those brothers were Saint Gregory of Nyssa and Saint Basil the Great, brilliant theologians and defenders of orthodox doctrine at the Council of Constantinople. Macrina taught them both through their boyhoods. Gregory, quiet and thoughtful, went on to study classical literature and philosophy; Basil, fiery and outspoken, studied law and rhetoric. Both ended up renouncing the careers their education had set them on, and seeking ordination.

The youngest brother, Peter, and Basil were cofounders of the monastery that corresponded to Macrina's convent, in the big villa inherited from their parents. Basil would later be appointed Bishop of Caesarea, two hundred miles to the south, where he founded a soup kitchen and a huge hospital/poorhouse, as well as preaching daily and taking the time to write sharply worded letters to politicians. (At one point, he more or less took over the administration of the city, much to the annoyance of his contemporary Eusebius.) But his heart remained in the community he'd founded with his siblings; Macrina's hospitality as well as her teaching had marked him for life.

(continued on preceding page)

Susannah Black is an editor of Plough *and has written for* First Things, Fare Forward, Front Porch Republic, Mere Orthodoxy, *and* The American Conservative. *She lives in New York City.* **Jason Landsel** *is the artist for* Plough's *"Forerunners" series, including the painting opposite.*